The American Indian

Edited by Norris Hundley, jr.
Foreword by Vine Deloria, Jr.

Essays from the PACIFIC HISTORICAL REVIEW by

Robert F. Berkhofer, Jr.   Nancy Oestreich Lurie

William T. Hagan   Donald L. Parman

Wilbur R. Jacobs   Wilcomb Washburn

CLIO BOOKS

AMERICAN BIBLIOGRAPHICAL CENTER—CLIO PRESS, INC.

SANTA BARBARA   OXFORD

Library of Congress Catalog Card Number 74–76443
ISBN PAPERBOUND EDITION 0-87436-140-0
ISBN CLOTHBOUND EDITION 0-87436-139-7

The articles by Wilcomb Washburn, Wilbur R. Jacobs, Nancy O. Lurie, William T. Hagan, Robert F. Berkhofer, Jr., and Donald L. Parman are reprinted here with the permission of the authors. The articles previously appeared in the *Pacific Historical Review,* Volume XL, No. 1 (February 1971) and Volume XL, No. 3 (August 1971).

Second printing, 1976

American Bibliographical Center—Clio Press, Inc.
2040 Alameda Padre Serra
Santa Barbara, California

European Bibliographical Center—Clio Press
Woodside House, Hinksey Hill
Oxford OX1 5BE, England

Composed in linotype Baskerville by
Kimberly Press Inc., Goleta, Calif.
Printed and bound by R. R. Donnelley
and Sons Co., Crawfordsville, Ind.
Cover design: Jack Swartz.

Contents

Foreword
  VINE DELORIA, JR.   vii

The Writing of American Indian History: A Status
Report
  WILCOMB WASHBURN   3

The Fatal Confrontation: Early Native-White Relations
on the Frontiers of Australia, New Guinea, and America
—A Comparative Study
  WILBUR R. JACOBS   27

The World's Oldest On-Going Protest Demonstration:
North American Indian Drinking Patterns
  NANCY OESTREICH LURIE   55

Kiowas, Comanches, and Cattlemen, 1867–1906: A
Case Study of the Failure of U.S. Reservation Policy
  WILLIAM T. HAGAN   77

The Political Context of a New Indian History
  ROBERT F. BERKHOFER, JR.   101

The Indian and the Civilian Conservation Corps
  DONALD L. PARMAN   127

Index   146

Foreword

ONE IS NOT OFTEN INVITED to write a foreword to a book that contains among its selections two articles where one's sins, alleged sins, anticipated sins—and perhaps highest goals—are discussed in the third person. It is a rare opportunity for mischief, but I will forbear. Being very good friends with Wilcomb Washburn and Nancy Lurie and a devoted admirer of Wilbur Jacobs places me in a difficult situation if I am to be a commentator and sometime critic. Since the Sioux style is to charge before the wagon train disperses, the following ensues.

Washburn's article is the first short article to give serious consideration to Indians as reflective beings. Not that a thousand anthologies have not recorded Chief Joseph's surrender speech, thereby establishing the Indian as poet. However, Washburn sees in recent efforts of such Indians as Scott Momaday and myself the perspective of contemporary Indian life redefined in un-Indian forms of expression. Part of that perspective is that we should no longer remain silent as non-Indian scholars hone and refine their definitions of "Indian." Several well-respected major publishing houses still search for the "as-told-to" book on Indians. Washburn attempts to provide a transitional interpretation of the emergence of Indian writers and Indian issues. It is debatable whether his colleagues will chastise him for calling me a writer or implying that I am a historian. The fact remains that Washburn continues to push his fellow historians toward the twentieth century. A Promethean task at best.

I could not have appreciated Wilbur Jacobs several years ago, and I suspect that many people will not today understand why his essay is included in this selection. His vision is far-flung, a generation ahead of both whites and Indians, and of my own acquaintances I can name only Chief George Manuel of Canada and Hank Adams of fishing rights fame (perhaps Thomas Banyaca of the Hopi) as individuals who have somehow intuited the necessity of linking the aboriginal peoples of the globe into a "fourth world" movement.

Jacobs's comparison of Australia, New Guinea, and the American frontiers is very important if one would understand the very new conception of the "fourth world." At a time in man's existence when the nation states of the world are making every effort to wipe tribal societies from the face of the earth, tribal men are reasserting their ancient traditions and community integrity. And these same nation states are suffering internal ruptures as their submerged minorities—the Bretons, Basques, Welsh, Flemish, and other groups—assert their national identities. Thus Jacobs's essay gives one possible format for understanding both the original people of the western and southern hemispheres and for viewing internal European national struggles in a new and more profound light.

Suffice it to say that Indians are sympathetic to the Irish struggle, view in the internal affairs of the South American and Central American countries the patterns of genocide, and express suspicion and disbelief at Canadian and Australian ventures in control of aboriginal peoples. Chief George Manuel has already visited the Lapps of Sweden and is planning a conference of aboriginal peoples to explore precisely those issues that Jacobs has raised.

Nancy Lurie and I have sparred over the years on a variety of issues, but outside the realm of ideas have remained close friends and allies in helping the Menominees and other tribes with the solution of their practical and pressing problems. Her essay on a theory to explain Indian drinking patterns is complex, controversial, and frequently attacked by myself for political purposes. What seems to me to obscure her theory is that it is written primarily for the academic world to force them to confront more than traditional categories of analysis. Yet when it appears within the Indian political context it makes us uncomfortable.

There is no denying that alcoholism is a problem. In 1970 we had a conference on alcoholism in Denver, and the keynote speaker who was to warn us against the evils of John Barleycorn was too drunk to make his presentation. In Nancy's reference to the absence of a drunken stereotype among poor whites and poor blacks, in effect undercutting the cherished liberal explanation of drinking as an escape from poverty, we have the beginnings of a fuller theory of Indian drinking patterns. I still feel that there is a direct correlation between the drinking of the educated younger Indians and the social science theory that people between two cultures are frustrated and drink to escape their dilemma. Regardless of whether the anthropologist serves as a convenient excuse for what would otherwise simply be irresponsibility or some other factor affecting modern Indians, Nancy's essay is a brave attempt to place the subject on a more sophisticated level of discussion.

William T. Hagan has an incisive mind and a command of his subject matter far greater than his contemporaries. I have always relied upon his writings when preparing testimony for appearances before congressional committees and in arguments involving the formation of federal policies. His essay is important, it seems to me, because it goes beyond the generalizations of Indian and western history with which we have become familiar in the writings of Chief Red Fox, Dee Brown, and Alvin Josephy, Jr.—whose writings are distinguishable from one another only in writing style and which give us no better picture of life in the old West than a good Clint Eastwood movie.

The oral tradition laid down by the militants at Wounded Knee in 1973 was a popularization of the old history which saw the United States government as the chief perpetrator of mischief toward the Indians. Hagan jolts us backwards to confront the situation. The game was, after all, cowboys and Indians, and as we learn about the nature of their confrontation on a specific reservation we see that the struggle for the West was largely local and desperate. Had the militants at Wounded Knee had one article such as this to read before they went on the rampage things might have been decidedly different and something might have been accomplished beside Marlon Brando forfeiting his Oscar in a fit of emotion.

Robert Berkhofer's essay troubles me in many ways. I find there an assumption that the history which has been written has somehow been adequate in its articulation although a failure because of the point of view which it has taken. I myself do not find that it has even focused on whites and the Indian-white relationship to any great degree. Instead, I find that it has shown an incredible fascination with one era, 1860–1890, and that it has confined itself to spinning even greater yarns about the wars with the Plains Indians. Beneath all of the rhetoric, we find in the histories already written a childish Hollywood point of view that sees in the dispossession of Indians an affirmation of American values even when the values are malevolent.

In recent months I have been stockpiling materials on the period 1860–1934 for eventual presentation to congressional committees with the hopes that we can get some major reforms enacted. What do I discover? Nothing significant written on the role of railroads in dispossessing Indians, little on the cattle barons and the Indian wars, virtually nothing on the timber barons and the cession of lands in the

Pacific Northwest, and not one decent comprehensive history of the period. Thus, instead of introducing another social science dimension into the articulation of history, we should really be honest and recognize that, despite all the majesty, power, and sadness that it invokes in us, the story of Chief Joseph has already been done. But what about James J. Hill, his railroad, and the Sioux wars? Nothing. That is the failure of contemporary historians. They want popularity and not truth.

That is why I choose to end this foreword with Donald Parman's article on the Indian and the Civilian Conservation Corps. Thank God somebody has understood that the CCC is far more important for this generation of Indians to understand than the number of warriors Red Cloud used at the Wagon Box fight or what Lewis and Clark had for breakfast in 1803 on the Yellowstone. The only memory that Indians in South Dakota had of good times was the days of the CCC. When the vaunted War on Poverty arrived on the reservations, the people wanted a return to the CCC because it reminded them of the only time that the reservation had a steady payroll. The Oglala Sioux created a "Ranger Corps" modeled partially on the CCC, and it was among the most successful programs of any Indian tribe. Not only did it bring a steady payroll, but it fell within the historical consciousness of the people and gave them a pride in themselves that was magnificent to behold.

This generation needs to know what experiences their elders have had, what federal policies have existed, what the Indian response to those policies was, and why things are the way they are. The problems of the Oglala Sioux may ultimately go back to the breach of the 1868 treaty; they more immediately go back to the federal leasing policy of 1917. Replacing the present tribal government with traditional chiefs, as the militants propose, will only complicate, not solve, the problems.

The articles in this book are important because they range into areas that are still relatively unknown to most people today. In many ways they call us to account for a basic honesty in social movement and federal policies, and such a call is uncomfortable at best. The Indian movement today is dangerously overcommitted to antiwhite sentiments because it does not understand its own history. The reaction of whites to the movement is equally overbalanced because of a frantic desire to obliterate historical fact by contending that such events as Sand Creek and Wounded Knee were not all that bad. But these articles give a dimension of hard reality to the slogans and sentiments of contemporary Indian life. If the red man must ride away into the sunset, at least let us do it driving an Oldsmobile 98, gloriously drunk, and remembering that the Australian aborigines have it much rougher over there.

VINE DELORIA, JR.

The Writing of American Indian History: A Status Report

WILCOMB WASHBURN

The author is director of American Studies in the Smith-sonian Institution.

N EARLY TWENTY YEARS AGO, in a conference on early American Indian and white relations sponsored by the Institute of Early American History and Culture at Williamsburg, Virginia, William N. Fenton looked forward to the day when an Institute for American Indian History and Culture might "arise from the smoke of prairie fires" with perhaps an L. H. Morgan chair in American ethnology and a Sequoia Press for American Indian languages. He even suggested forming a new conspiracy to promote a Pontiac lectureship in American Indian history. The era hoped for by Fenton has not yet arrived but we have, nevertheless, come a long way toward the goal. The writing of American Indian history is thriving. Organizations for those involved in the writing of Indian history have been formed. Indian studies programs have been established at a number of universities. True, much of the impetus for the recent support of Indian studies comes not for historical but for racial reasons. Nevertheless, the movement is, I think, a healthy one, and one that will not die with the waning of racial animosities or concern.

Because of the wide diversity and varied histories of the numerous "tribes, bands, or other identifiable groups of American Indians" (to use the catchall phraseology of the Indian Claims Commission Act), the bulk of the ethnographic and historical literature on the American Indian is devoted to individual tribes rather than to the Indian or to Indian-white relations generally. I will cite a few examples of such works—those primarily historical in content—written by both historians and ethnologists. My main concern will be, however, to suggest trends in the writing of Indian history that seem evident amidst the mountains of literature being produced, and to comment upon several problems that bedevil the enterprise.

The first and greatest problem concerns the possibility of writing a good general history of the American Indian. I think it fair to say that no historian has yet succeeded in producing an unchallengeable model. (Whether any anthropologist has succeeded in the same quest will be considered later in this essay.) A recent attempt at a general history of the American Indian is Alvin M. Josephy, Jr.'s *The Indian Heritage of America* (New York, Alfred A. Knopf, 1968).[1] For all its many virtues, it is perhaps too encyclopedic to create a single impression in the mind of the reader. Peter Farb's *Man's Rise to Civilization as Shown by the Indians of North America from Primeval Times to the Coming of the Industrial State* (New York, E. P. Dutton & Co., 1968) is more selective and reflects the author's imaginative concern with problems of broad popular interest (e.g., the Eskimo's adaptation to his environment, the Iroquois' primitive democracy). A weakness of Farb's book is its uncritical acceptance of the theory of cultural evolution enunciated by Elman R. Service, Leslie A. White, and others. Indeed, Service's foreword to the book makes rather extravagant claims for the extent of Farb's contribution to the theory and practice of cultural evolution, which, in Service's words, "holds that the origin of the major divergent forms of culture are functional concomitants of the rise of societal complexity—that is, of the evolutionary process itself." Both Josephy and Farb appeal to the general reader though their work is soundly based in the scholarly literature.

Another writer whose work is based on scholarly research but who writes for the general reader is William Brandon, author of the narrative for *The American Heritage Book of Indians* (New York, 1961, and issued in paperback by Bantam Books, 1964), by the editors of *American Heritage*, under the general editorship of Alvin M. Josephy, Jr. Angie Debo's recent *A History of the Indians of the United States* (Norman, University of Oklahoma Press, 1970) demonstrates that the author's earlier successful accounts of the "Five Civilized Tribes" and of their removal to Oklahoma are no guarantee of her ability to handle

---

[1] References to books in *PHR* ordinarily omit the names of publishers. An exception has been made in this article because readers may wish to purchase the books cited.

the intractable problems of a general history of the Indian in the United States.

D'Arcy McNickle, a Flathead Indian who is a historian teaching in an anthropology department in Canada, has written a series of slim volumes giving a general overview of the history of Indian-white relations. Beginning in 1949 with *They Came Here First: The Epic of the American Indian* (Philadelphia, Lippincott) and continuing with *Indians and Other Americans: Two Ways of Life Meet*, in conjunction with Harold E. Fey (New York, Harper & Row, 1959, rev. ed., 1970) and *The Indian Tribes of the United States: Ethnic and Cultural Survival* (London, Oxford University Press, 1962, issued under the auspices of the Institute of Race Relations), McNickle has provided a valuable general—though not detailed—guide to the entire range of Indian history. William T. Hagan's brief survey, *American Indians*, in the Chicago History of American Civilization series (Chicago, University of Chicago Press, 1961) is an admirable essay on the course of Indian-white relations in the United States. Chronology is its major organizing principle and brevity its dominating characteristic.

Despite these examples, I think it is fair to say that the tantalizing possibility of a successful general history of the American Indian remains unfulfilled. While historians have failed at the task of producing a synthesis, many have succeeded admirably in dealing with specific tribes during specific eras. One can do no more than cite a few examples from the recent past, among which are William T. Hagan's *The Sac and Fox Indians* (Norman, University of Oklahoma Press, 1958), James C. Olson's *Red Cloud and the Sioux Problem* (Lincoln, University of Nebraska Press, 1965), Arrell M. Gibson's *The Kickapoos: Lords of the Middle Border* (Norman, University of Oklahoma Press, 1963), and Alvin M. Josephy, Jr.'s *The Nez Perce Indians and the Opening of the Northwest* (New Haven and London, Yale University Press, 1965). Individual studies by anthropologists writing as historians will be alluded to later in this essay, but no attempt will be made to survey this literature as a whole. All such studies add to our fund of knowledge about different groups of Indians and are the building blocks upon which a future successful general history will have to be based.

Humanistically-oriented historians—more so than scientifically trained anthropologists—have tended to think in moral terms in their consideration of Indian-white relationships. Yet one finds among historians of this relationship two opposing schools. Among those who have tended to emphasize what they regard as a continuing pattern of unjust or unconscionable actions by the federal government (and its predecessor colonial governments) in its dealings with Indians are Wilbur Jacobs, William T. Hagan, and myself. Among those who tend to emphasize purer motives and more honorable dealings on the part of the whites are Francis Paul Prucha, Alden Vaughan, and Douglas Leach.

Outstanding among the group whose interpretation tends to be oriented toward the government point of view is Francis Paul Prucha, whose thorough study of *American Indian Policy in the Formative Years: The Indian Trade and Intercourse Acts, 1790–1834* (Cambridge, Harvard University Press, 1962) was the outcome of his graduate work at Harvard. In another place I have tried to show that Father Prucha's book is flawed by too trusting an attitude toward the expressed verbal or written views of the federal government and by too perfunctory a consideration of federal actions which failed to live up to professions of concern for the rights and welfare of the American Indian.[2]

Prucha's ability to see the best motives in what others regard as a bad cause was most startlingly evident in his paper on "Andrew Jackson's Indian Policy: A Reassessment," given at the 1968 meeting of the Western History Association and published later in the *Journal of American History*.[3] When delivered at Tucson, the paper was greeted with incredulity by some of the audience. One, indeed, thought that Prucha, in his defense of the sincerity and purity of Jackson's attitude toward the Indians, was talking with tongue in cheek. Prucha's cool, apparently dispassionate critique of United States Indian policy, particularly when delivered by someone in a clerical collar, infuriates those non-clerical moralists who believe they see more clearly into the hearts of men than does Father Prucha. While presenting a strong case against the claimed excesses of his opponents' "devil theory" of American Indian policy, as he calls it, Prucha substitutes what his opponents might claim to be an unrealistic "angel theory" in its stead. Prucha is presently working on a history of United States

---

2 Wilcomb E. Washburn, "Indian Removal Policy: Administrative, Historical and Moral Criteria for Judging its Success or Failure," *Ethnohistory*, XII (1965), 274–278.

3 *Journal of American History*, LVI (1969), 527–539.

government relations with the Indians in the last half of the nineteenth century, and has recently prepared for the press an impressive study of the manufacture and use of Indian peace medals.

Alden T. Vaughan of Columbia University, in his *New England Frontier: Puritans and Indians, 1620–1675* (Boston and Toronto, Little, Brown and Co., 1965), concluded, after a thorough investigation of the sources, that "the New England Puritans followed a remarkably humane, considerate, and just policy in their dealings with the Indians."[4] Vaughan's sympathetic treatment of the colonial New England authorities has aroused a reaction similar to that elicited by Father Prucha's defense of federal Indian policy. Not that the conflict is new. Historians from the seventeenth century to the present day have argued bitterly about the causes and effects, facts and interpretations, and rights and wrongs of the Pequot War and King Philip's War in New England. Indeed, a recent article has thrown new light on the bitter feud between Increase Mather and William Hubbard, whose conflicting histories of King Philip's War were prepared for the press in 1676, even while the war raged.[5] The interpretation of the events of that time is especially difficult because the bulk of the information comes from English sources alone. Those sources express not only hard facts but also vague fears, rumors, and justifications for actions taken. If the "sources" available are sympathetically accepted by latter-day historians, one can justify the Pequot War and King Philip's War historically in the same manner that the English colonial authorities justified their military actions against the natives in the seventeenth century. If, on the other hand, one examines these sources with a skeptical or, as I would urge, with a judicial eye, it is possible to question the motives as well as the understanding and judgment of the English. I have done so in my review of Douglas Leach's *Flintlock and Tomahawk: New England in King Philip's War* (New York, Macmillan, 1958), in which I point out the questionable assumptions upon which the English based their belief in a conspiracy by King Philip.[6] The fact that the first blood in the war was drawn by the English is only one of the many curious circumstances of this costliest of America's Indian wars.

---

4 Preface, p. vii.

5 Anne Kusener Nelsen, "King Philip's War and the Hubbard-Mather Rivalry," *William and Mary Quarterly*, XXVII (1970), 615–629.

6 *Pennsylvania Magazine of History and Biography*, LXXXII (1958), 473–474.

Even in his later book, *The Northern Colonial Frontier, 1607–1763* (New York, Holt, Rinehart and Winston, 1966), in which he makes a conscious attempt to consider the importance of cultural differences, Leach tends to think ethnically rather than judicially in recounting the events of King Philip's War. Thus we are told that the war broke out when Wampanoag warriors began looting houses in the frontier town of Swansea, thirty miles west of Plymouth. "Looting was followed by killing; both Plymouth and Massachusetts hurried militiamen to the scene; and the most bloody Indian war of the seventeenth century was under way." Leach identifies those who began the looting but not those who began the killing. The reader might imagine that the Indians were at fault in both cases. Similarly, Leach postulates a "spirit of defiance" on the part of King Philip which "tribe after tribe" soon caught and then joined "the war of extermination against the white men."[7] No judge reviewing the evidence today would jump to so easy a conclusion.

The American Indian has attracted, in addition to historians and anthropologists, numerous intellectual and literary historians who have seen him as part of the New World context within which transplanted Europeans had to function physically, intellectually, and spiritually. The literary tradition is a glorious one, stretching back to such giants as Montaigne, Rousseau, and D. H. Lawrence. Among American scholars who have recently analyzed the meaning of the American Indian in the mind of the white man, the foremost is Roy Harvey Pearce. Pearce's *The Savages of America: A Study of the Indian and the Idea of Civilization* (Baltimore, Johns Hopkins University Press, 1953) was issued in a revised edition in 1965. The Indian, in Pearce's analysis, evoked in the mind of the transplanted European both the memory of the savage heritage from which he—the white man—had emerged and the consciousness of the continuing savage obstacles which he had to overcome in order to create a civilization worthy of the name on the western shores of the Atlantic.

Henry Nash Smith, in his classic *Virgin Land: The American West as Symbol and Myth*, first printed in 1950 by Harvard University Press, and Leo Marx in his *The Machine in the Garden: Technology and the Pastoral Ideal in America* (New York, Oxford University Press, 1964), particularly in his essay on "Shakespeare's American

---

7 Leach, *Northern Colonial Frontier*, 56.

Fable," have similarly delved into the consequences of Europe's exposure to America's "savage" background. In the view of these scholars of literature, the Indian is scarcely distinguishable from the natural landscape, yet he suffuses it and it him and both the transplanted European. Another essay in this rich literary field is Howard Mumford Jones' *O Strange New World: American Culture—The Formative Years* (New York, Viking Press, 1964) which, however, displays more bombast and pedantry than true insight.

The most recent literary examination of the impact of the Indian upon the white psyche is Leslie A. Fiedler's *The Return of the Vanishing American* (New York, Stein and Day, 1968). Fiedler's book is less about the Indian than about the European settler who confronted him, attempted to convert him, corrupted him, and eventually destroyed him. It is the image of the Vanishing American, as Fiedler puts it, that has "haunted all Americans, in their dreams at least if not in their waking consciousness; for it is rooted in our profoundest guilt: our awareness that we began our national life by killing something vital to the New World as well as something essential to the Old. . . ."[8] After conducting the reader on an erudite tour of the impact of the Indian on the American imagination (his discussion of the Pocahontas story is especially perceptive), Fiedler concludes with the plea that our writers engage in a dialogue with the leaders of the new drug culture who, he suggests, may have inherited the mantle of the Indians as the keeper of "a myth of America" that is essential to our continued existence.

Among the younger breed of analysts of the impact of the Indian on the "mind" of America is Bernard Sheehan, whose doctoral dissertation on "Civilization and the American Indian in the Thought of the Jeffersonian Era" (University of Virginia, 1965) is currently being revised for publication. Sheehan's point of view has been well expressed in an article entitled "Indian-White Relations in Early America: A Review Essay" and amplified in another article on "Paradise and the Noble Savage in Jeffersonian Thought."[9] Seeking to avoid the charge of romanticizing the Indian, he has assumed a hard-nosed attitude toward any view of Indians of the past which is not

---

[8] Fiedler, *Return of the Vanishing American*, 75.

[9] "Indian-White Relations in Early America: A Review Essay," *William and Mary Quarterly*, XXVI (1969), 267–286; "Paradise and the Noble Savage in Jeffersonian Thought," *ibid.*, 327–359.

consistent with his own unromantic assumptions. His views seem to be derived from a Europe-centered value system against which the character and behavior of Indians—both present-day and past—are unconsciously judged. Though he gives lip service to the notion of cultural analysis, he assumes what is to be proved: that the historical Indian was without the special qualities—variously perceived on a value spectrum ranging from diabolical to angelic—often attributed to him. Given his assumptions, anyone who thinks differently—anyone who "romanticizes" the Indian—is wrong. The problem of the nature of the historical Indian is much more complicated than Sheehan assumes and one can expect that the subject will continue to occupy him and other scholars in the years to come. Writers in the literary tradition would do well to consider the anthropologist Alfred Irving Hallowell's classic essay on "The Backwash of the Frontier: The Impact of the Indian on American Culture," in Walker D. Wyman and Clifton B. Kroeber, eds., *The Frontier in Perspective* (Madison, University of Wisconsin Press, 1957).

The most striking feature concerning the writing of Indian history in recent times, however, has been the emergence of the professional anthropologist as historian. Institutionally the study of the native American has become increasingly a function of the anthropology departments rather than of history departments. Because of the decline of traditional Indian cultures and the growing assimilation of the American Indian into the larger American society, any study of the Indian's distinct past must increasingly take on the character of history or sociology rather than of classical ethnography. Yet history departments are not moving to establish their concern in this field. Indeed, some young historians have been discouraged from going into the field. Anthropologists, on the other hand, are expanding their functions in this area, as they are in archeology, where anthropology departments are turning out more and more historical archeologists whose dissertations are in the field of colonial history rather than on prehistoric Indian sites. The anthropologist brings to his study both strengths and weaknesses. The principal strength he brings to the subject is his training in acute observation of behavior, his habit of seeing particular cultures in terms of a theoretical framework, and his ability to divest himself of his own cultural presuppositions and values in recording and analyzing the culture he is studying. Neither the anthropologist nor any other human can entirely divest himself of his own prejudices—witness the fact of, and furor caused by, the publication of Bronislaw Malinowski's *A Diary in the Strict Sense of the Term*, translated by Norbert Guterman (New York, Harcourt, Brace & World, 1967), in which Malinowski's loathing for "the niggers," as he describes the Trobrianders and other Papuans he studied, is recounted to the distress of anthropologists, reviewers, and, presumably, Malinowski's memory. Ian Hogbin, reviewing the book in the *American Anthropologist*, asserted that "the volume holds no interest for anyone, be he anthropologist, psychologist, student of biography, or merely a gossip."[10] Despite this embarrassing revelation of an anthropologist's failure to produce a diary free of value-judgments, the fact remains that anthropologists are trained to discriminate between their own values and those of their subjects.

The road by which anthropologists have become historians is illustrated by the career of Wendell H. Oswalt. Oswalt's doctoral dissertation in anthropology at the University of Arizona in 1959 was based on fieldwork in the Alaskan Eskimo community of Napaskiak prior to 1956. In his dissertation, published as *Napaskiak: An Alaskan Eskimo Community* (Tucson, University of Arizona Press, 1963), Oswalt noted the prevalent tendency to romanticize the Eskimo by dealing with him in terms of what his life may have been. "Virtually every popular contemporary account," he wrote, "maximizes aboriginal survivals."[11] Oswalt, in contrast, attempted to describe the 141 Eskimos he studied in "his" community along the Kuskokwim River exactly as he found them in 1956. His commitment to describing the unheroic character of his subjects' day-to-day life leads him, in his chapter on "Family Life," to record the following actions of a typical man on a typical day in December:

About 8:00 A.M. the man, wearing cotton long underwear, wakes, sits on the edge of the bed, and then crosses the room to one of the windows. Scratching a bit of the frost away from the pane with his fingernail, he looks out to see what the weather is like; then he glances at the thermometer attached to the outside of the window.[12]

As Oswalt continued his study of the Eskimo villagers along the Kuskokwim, he turned increasingly from the ethnographic present (of

---

10 *American Anthropologist*, LXX (1968), 575.
11 Oswalt, *Napaskiak*, v.
12 *Ibid.*, 17.

1956) to the historical past left in the records of Russian traders and administrators, of the Greek Church, and, after Alaska was acquired by the United States, of the Moravian Church. As Oswalt put it in the introduction to his *Mission of Change in Alaska: Eskimos and Moravians on the Kuskokwim* (San Marino, Huntington Library, 1963),

Finally [after studying the Kuskokwim people in 1950, 1953, 1955–56, and 1960], I realized that no matter how many people I questioned, much of the knowledge of the aboriginal past was lost to memory. The only hope for gathering additional information seemed to lie in discovering pertinent historical records. . . .[13]

Professor Oswalt's technical skill in amalgamating the ethnographic and historical record of one group was applied by him to the study of ten diverse tribes (including the Kuskokwim Eskimo) in his *This Land Was Theirs: A Study of the North American Indian* (New York, John Wiley & Sons, 1966). In this book Oswalt attempted to write the history of the American Indian by selecting specific tribes to represent each culture area of North America. Oswalt tells their several stories, in non-theoretical terms, both as historical summaries of their past and as descriptions of their "traditional" way of life. The result is partially successful, though one gets the chronologies and descriptions of several Indian tribes side by side with no attempt to generalize except in a concluding chapter in which the legal status of present-day Indians is outlined.

Harold E. Driver, professor of anthropology at Indiana University and author of *Indians of North America* (Chicago, University of Chicago Press, 1961, 2d ed., rev., 1969), is another of the anthropologists who have increasingly adapted historical materials to their purpose. Driver's work is organized as a comprehensive and detailed consideration of the material and social culture of the American Indian. One of its distant ancestors is Clark Wissler's *Indians of the United States*, first published in 1940, and recently reprinted in a revised edition prepared by Lucy Wales Kluckhohn (Garden City, New York, Doubleday, 1966). Wissler emphasized the material culture of the American Indian above all else, though he made some generalizations about non-material culture. In Wissler's book, history, when it emerges at all, tends to be anecdotal in character. Driver, on the other hand, has

---

[13] Oswalt, *Mission of Change*, vii–viii.

adopted a more comprehensive ethnological approach and, in addition, has made a more conscious effort to achieve a historical perspective. The last chapter of the first edition of his *Indians of North America* has been deleted in the second edition and five new chapters on ethnohistory and culture-change after 1492 added. Nevertheless, Driver's historical chapters tend to be rather wooden recitals of basic facts which stand in uneasy contrast to the earlier chapters where he carefully analyzes housing, architecture, clothing, marriage, the family, and other topics. Driver's continent-wide topical approach is faulted by some anthropologists who see it as unhistorical in contrast to the areal and tribal organization of other recent general volumes on North American Indians.

Another anthropologist who has turned increasingly to history, after doing traditional ethnographic field work and producing studies in acculturation and applied anthropology, is Edward H. Spicer, whose *Cycles of Conquest: The Impact of Spain, Mexico, and the United States on the Indians of the Southwest, 1533–1960* (Tucson, University of Arizona Press, 1962) dealt with one segment of the Indian population in one section of the United States. More recently, Spicer has published *A Short History of the Indians of the United States* (New York, Van Nostrand Reinhold Co., 1969) which combines documents and commentary in a compressed and readable form. Spicer decries the fact that Indian history is too often merely the record of Indian-white relations and points out that Indian societies, even under the impact of white-induced change, are nevertheless still distinctly Indian societies whose continuity with the past should be recognized. Still, in searching for an organizing principle for his history, Spicer divides his book into chronological segments based on the legal standing of Indian societies and Indian individuals within the context of an increasingly dominant white society.

While nobody has solved the problem of producing a meaningful general history of the American Indian, perhaps the anthropologists have come closest. In addition to the books by Driver, Spicer, and Oswalt, a team of anthropologists (Robert F. Spencer, Jesse D. Jennings, and a number of other specialists) has produced a college textbook, *The Native Americans* (New York, Harper & Row, 1965). This volume, although written in ethnological rather than historical terms and following the culture-area approach, uses historical evidence to illustrate the ethnographic points made. The authors also make good use of archeological materials in sketching the prehistory of the American Indian. A forthcoming example of the team approach to the study of American Indian history, scheduled for publication late in 1971, is *North American Indians in Historical Perspective*, edited by Nancy O. Lurie and Eleanor Leacock, which will include chapters on areas and tribes by a number of different authors. Perhaps the team approach is the only way possible to encompass the ethnographic diversity and historical complexity of Indian history.

A number of anthropologists have focussed their talents on specific tribes for which the historical record rather than ethnographic fieldwork provides the bulk of their data. The writings of certain of these anthropologists is, perhaps, distinguishable from the work of traditional historians only by the richer depth of understanding of their Indian subjects that they bring to their work. One of the most outstanding anthropologists writing as historian is Anthony F. C. Wallace. Working within the well-documented period of Indian-white relations in Pennsylvania and New York in the eighteenth and early nineteenth centuries, Wallace has been able to bring the "culture-and-personality" approach of anthropology to the study of critical periods and key individuals in the Indian-white relationship. He described his first book, *King of the Delawares: Teedyuscung, 1700–1763* (Philadelphia, University of Pennsylvania Press, 1949, reprinted, 1970) as

not simply an historical treatise, or an ethnographical one; it is also, and primarily, a biography. As such it deals in discussions of emotions, motives, and states of mind—intangible matters, indeed, but the stuff of which a life is made—which lie outside the province of the pure historian or ethnographer.[14]

There followed a string of brilliant technical articles in a wide variety of anthropological, scientific, and historical journals. Most recently, in *The Death and Rebirth of the Seneca: The History and Culture of the Great Iroquois Nation, their Destruction and Demoralization, and their Cultural Revival at the Hands of the Indian Visionary, Handsome Lake* (New York, Alfred A. Knopf, 1970), Wallace demonstrated how effectively the anthropological, psychological, and historical approaches can be welded together. The book's subtitle (which is placed opposite the title page but immediately under the title on the

---

14 Wallace, *King of the Delawares*, vii.

book jacket) reflects not only a trend in contemporary book titling techniques, but accurately reflects the amalgam of Anglo-American history, Indian tribal culture, and individual psychology, which it is Wallace's genius to be able to combine in readable form. The first part of Wallace's book sets the stage for the last part by establishing the cultural assumptions and practices of the Senecas. Then we are given a chronological account of the decline of Seneca power followed by a description of the renaissance induced by the teachings of Handsome Lake. Wallace's task is easier than that of the historian or anthropologist attempting to tell the story of all Indians, but within the limits of the one tribe he has isolated, Wallace and his research assistant, Sheila C. Steen, have done a superb job of writing Indian history.

Two other anthropologists have distinguished themselves by the impetus they have given to ethnohistorical study. John C. Ewers has produced a staggering array of historical studies illuminated by a deep personal and professional knowledge of Plains Indians. One might cite his *The Blackfeet: Raiders on the Northwestern Plains* (Norman, University of Oklahoma Press, 1958) as an example. William N. Fenton, during a lifetime of work with the Iroquois of New York State, has made fundamental contributions to our understanding of them and of their dealings with the whites from the seventeenth century to the present. In addition to his anthropological writings, Fenton has edited Lewis Henry Morgan's *League of the Iroquois* (New York, Corinth Books, 1962) as well as Arthur C. Parker's notes on the Iroquois, *Parker on the Iroquois* (Syracuse, University of Syracuse Press, 1968), and has in preparation an English language edition of Joseph-Francois Lafitau's *Moeurs des sauvages amériquains* (Paris, 1724).

Among anthropologists concerned with the American Indian are several who are themselves Indians. Two of the most distinguished are Alfonso Ortiz, associate professor of anthropology at Princeton University, who has recently published *The Tewa World: Space, Time, Being and Becoming in a Pueblo Society* (Chicago, University of Chicago Press, 1969), and the late Edward P. Dozier who has written on the Pueblos, as in his *Hano: A Tewa Community in Arizona* (New York, Holt, Rinehart & Winston, 1966). Both Ortiz and Dozier are themselves Pueblo by birth and upbringing. Though writing primarily as anthropologists rather than as historians, their work—especially Dozier's—can be classified as ethnohistory because of its extensive reliance upon the record of the past—a record which reveals the remarkable continuity shown by Pueblo society in the face of successive challenges from both Indian and non-Indian forces.

The evidence of the surge of historical interest within the anthropological profession flows from the presses with increasing frequency. A recent example is Robert F. Heizer and Alan J. Almquist's *The Other Californians: Prejudice and Discrimination under Spain, Mexico, and the United States to 1920* (Berkeley, University of California Press, 1971). Almquist, a doctoral candidate in anthropology at the University of California, Berkeley, began this essentially historical study as a seminar paper. The powerful nature of his findings encouraged his professor, Robert Heizer, to effect the collaboration that resulted in the present book. From the historian's point of view the book commits an error for which history students are often faulted: excessive use of lengthy quotation from the sources. From the anthropological point of view, these quotations—undigested—are of more value to the anthropologist (because they provide source material for future anthropological analysis) than a fully digested historical analysis would be.

The trend to history among North American anthropologists was institutionalized early in the 1950s by the creation of the American Indian Ethnohistoric Conference (more recently called the American Society for Ethnohistory) which publishes the journal, *Ethnohistory*. One need not enter the debate over whether "ethnohistory" is new or old, or whether it is a discipline or not, to point out that it marks an increasingly close amalgamation of the historical and the ethnographic approaches to the study of the American Indian. From the historian's point of view, it is regrettable that most of the amalgamation is being performed by anthropologists and very little by historians.

An irritant to historians is the tendency of some anthropologists to date the serious study of the American Indian from the establishment of anthropology as a formal academic discipline in the late nineteenth century. The effects of this narrow professionalism are seen in the shocked surprise registered by anthropologists at discovering anthropological principles adumbrated centuries before the rise of professional anthropology. Thomas B. Hinton, associate professor in the department of anthropology at the University of Arizona, in a review of Joseph-Marie Degérando's *The Observation of Savage Peoples*, translated from the French and edited by F. C. T. Moore (Berkeley,

University of California Press, 1969), confessed to "the vaguely uncomfortable feelings that this little volume stirs in the modern ethnol-
ogist." In the work, written in 1800 by a French philosopher, Hinton
observed that

We see an impressive number of techniques, viewpoints, and concepts virtually identical with those so laboriously developed by anthropologists
over more than a century of trial and error but which in this case were apparently easily formulated before anthropology began by a writer from
another discipline.[15]

Perhaps the only aspect of the study of native peoples in which the
historian rather than the anthropologist is taking the lead is in the
history of the discipline of anthropology. Anthropologists, like other
scientists, have until recently been unconcerned about or unable
adequately to record or to analyze their own history. Traditionally
trained historians have moved in to do the job. In the field of anthropology that role has been assumed by George Stocking, Jr., whose essays on the subject have been collected and published under the title
Race, Culture, and Evolution: Essays in the History of Anthropology
(New York, Free Press, 1968). Stocking has generated great interest in
the field among anthropologists who are now turning increasingly to
the study of the past history of their discipline.

A word might be said about comparative analysis as it appears in
such books as Howard Peckham and Charles Gibson, eds., *Attitudes
of Colonial Powers Toward the American Indian* (Salt Lake City,
University of Utah Press, 1969). Though designed as an attempt to
make a comparative analysis of the Indian relations of the different
European powers, the book gives us little more than a series of essays
on separate Indian policies and practices of the several European nations. The comparative analysis has yet to be accomplished. Anthropological attempts at comparative analysis have been more successful,
perhaps because of the existence within the anthropological community of an agreed-upon set of categories and a distinct method for
analyzing Indian cultures. An excellent example is the volume edited
by Edward H. Spicer and entitled *Perspectives in American Indian
Culture Change* (Chicago, University of Chicago Press, 1960), which
includes studies in the acculturation of six Indian tribes by six differ-

---

15 *Science*, CLXVIII (1970), 108.

ent anthropologists. One of the contributors is Edward Dozier, who deals with Rio Grande Pueblo contact-history in five successive stages.

What is the reason for the difficulties that seem to dog the professional historian and anthropologist writing about the Indian? Robert K. Berkhofer, Jr., has asserted in his *A Behavioral Approach to Historical Analysis* (New York, Free Press, 1969) that at the heart of the problem is the practical difficulty of reconciling a functional (synchronic) analysis of a whole culture with a historical (diachronic) analysis of the cumulative changes producing that culture. The "apparent impossibility" and "incompatibility" of "treating time as setting and as sequence simultaneously" is the historian's equivalent, Berkhofer suggests, of the natural scientist's principle of indeterminancy.[16] Berkhofer himself attempted to overcome the difficulty in his earlier *Protestant Missions and American Indian Response, 1787–1862* (Lexington, University of Kentucky Press, 1965). In this book he organized his data on Protestant denominations operating in the mission field into sequences starting with the missionaries' general attitudes and assumptions, and ending with the Indians' response to the missionary. Observing the regularities in these sequences, and applying a comparative approach to the vast sum of data before him, Berkhofer attempted to avoid the "usual moral fables that masquerade as Indian history."[17] His monograph does point to methods that should be applied by the historian in the study of Indian history, but traditional historians may assert that Berkhofer has applied a new terminology to well recognized historical, not alone sociological or anthropological, categories.

The contribution of the Indian to the writing of Indian history has been minimal. Vast stores of knowledge have been lost with the death of older Indians whose recollections were never recorded on tape or on paper. Though late in the day, it is still possible to tap this source. Of primary importance is the preservation of the original document side-by-side with the ethnographic or historical commentary. Specialized studies, such as Anna Gritts Kilpatrick and Jack Frederick Kilpatrick's "Chronicles of Wolftown" and "Notebook of a Cherokee Shaman," exemplify the respect that such documents deserve and ob-

---

16 Berkhofer, *A Behaviorial Approach*, 235–237.
17 Berkhofer, *Protestant Missions and American Indian Response,* xiv.

tain at the hands of sympathetic and scholarly observers.[18] Stanley Vestal, in a previous generation, had felt a similar compulsion to publish many of the documents and statements of Indian and white eyewitnesses to the events he discussed in his biography of Sitting Bull. Vestal's documentary, *New Sources of Indian History, 1850–1891, The Ghost Dance, The Prairie Sioux: A Miscellany* (Norman, University of Oklahoma Press, 1934), contained these fragments which, Vestal felt, were too valuable to cast aside after he had utilized them for his biography. In addition, Vestal provided an important prefatory note to the second part of his book describing his techniques of interviewing Indian informants.

A recent attempt to utilize Indian recollections to tell the history of native Americans is *Cheyenne Memories*, by John Stands in Timber and Margot Liberty, with the assistance of Robert M. Utley (New Haven and London, Yale University Press, 1967). In this book, the recollections of the Cheyennes' "historian" were taped, sorted, and annotated by sympathetic whites to form the "memories" of the published volume. The reader of these memories is, however, left without the knowledge of the original, whose preservation it is the primary responsibility of the historian to ensure. The preservation of the original tapes is, in this context, the equivalent of the responsibility owed by the author of any scholarly work to facilitate the reexamination of the original material by whoever may be skeptical of the interpretation the author has drawn from the material. Whether this responsibility has been met by the friends of the Cheyennes' historian is open to question. It is perhaps easier to ensure the preservation of the original material in the case of graphic documents. The preservation and analysis of a fascinating graphic account of Indian life has been effected by Karen Daniels Petersen and John C. Ewers in their edition of *Howling Wolf: A Cheyenne Warrior's Graphic Interpretation of His People* (Palo Alto, California, American West Publishing Co., 1968).

The urge to discover how Indians view their history is now *de rigueur* among foundations, universities, and government officials. Yet Indian history from the Indian point of view is not an easy goal to

---

18 "Chronicles of Wolftown: Social Documents of the North Carolina Cherokees, 1850–1862," *Anthropological Paper No. 75, Bureau of American Ethnology Bulletin No. 196* (Washington, 1966), 1–111; "Notebook of a Cherokee Shaman," *Smithsonian Contributions to Anthropology*, II (1970).

achieve. Though oral history has gained new respectability and oral history projects dealing with the Indian have been set up in several universities in the United States, important questions remain. Can these materials be translated into formal history? Can they provide us with true and significant insights into the Indian past? Oral history as derived from contemporaries who played major roles in history (e.g., generals and politicians in the post-World War II era) or from those individuals of whatever stature who knew a deceased figure of importance (e.g., those interviewed by T. Harry Williams in preparing his biography of Huey Long) can be demonstrated to be of immediate value in providing both the raw material of formal history and support for its interpretation. Oral interviews with contemporary Indians will certainly illuminate the condition of the present-day Indian and the story of his immediate past. In addition, it will record the Indian's perception of the history of his more distant past. Such interviews should be fundamental to the writing of both folk history and formal history, but their use for these purposes has not been fully demonstrated.

The voice of the Indian about his own history has recently been heard more clearly, though the use of whites as spokesmen for or collaborators with Indians has continued as in such books as Stan Steiner's _The New Indians_ (New York, Harper & Row, 1968). Billed as "the first full-scale report of the gathering 'Red Power' movement," the book professed to speak for the newly militant but still silent Indians. It did so, though Steiner suffered criticism from Indians who resented the fact that a white man took it upon himself, however selflessly, to speak for them. Steiner's book perhaps stimulated the direct expression of an Indian point of view by Indians. One of the first such expressions was Vine Deloria, Jr.'s _Custer Died for Your Sins_ (New York and London, Macmillan, 1969). Deloria's book marks the emergence of a group of Indian commentators on the Indian experience who self-consciously identify themselves not as anthropologists or as historians but as Indians. So far, this movement is more a matter of promise than of performance, but I, for one, am confident that the coming generation of Indians will advance the cause both of their race and of history.[19] Deloria's book is a wild swipe at the big, bad white world of

---

[19] Editor's note: An attempt was made to see that Indian scholars were represented in the pages of this issue. Though unsuccessful, our inquiries revealed that the number of Indian scholars interested in their history is large and growing.

anthropologists, missionaries, government functionaries, and last, but not least, Indian leaders themselves. All get a roasting which seems more ceremonial than real, more tongue-in-cheek than bitter. It is a curious form of contemporary history, justificatory and expiatory in its intent, as the title would indicate, and relying on the well-known guilt feelings of twentieth-century whites in order to be palatable to its targets.

Deloria's second book, *We Talk, You Listen: New Tribes, New Turf* (New York and Toronto, Macmillan, 1970), followed on the heels of *Custer*, even while the latter (and Deloria) was becoming the subject of several heated sessions at the American Anthropological Association's 1970 annual meeting. *We Talk, You Listen* expresses Deloria's search for a positive philosophy—based on the potential autonomy of the tribal unit—to replace the fallen idols of his past. Noticeable again in Deloria's rhetoric is his intense preoccupation with morality—an apparent carry-over from his days as a theological student—as well as his zeal for practical legal solutions—a reflection of his legal training and work as executive secretary of the National Congress of American Indians. *Custer Died for Your Sins* is the kind of book one writes to purge oneself. *We Talk, You Listen* begins the process of building a personal philosophy, though it still reflects the bitterness of Deloria's disillusionment with the philosophies in which he was raised. Deloria is not a historian in the traditional sense, but he gives Indians a voice and the belief that history can be written by Indians as well as by whites.

Some well-known Indians have approached their history through literature rather than through history, anthropology, or opinion. Most prominent among them is N. Scott Momaday, professor at the University of California, Berkeley, whose novel, *House of Dawn* (New York, Harper & Row, 1968), received the Pulitzer Prize for Fiction in 1969. Momaday has looked back to, and tried to evoke the essence of his Kiowa heritage in such works as *The Journey of Tai-me* (Santa Barbara, University of California Press, 1967) and *The Way to Rainy Mountain* (Albuquerque, University of New Mexico Press, 1969). While the approach to Indian history through literature will always be insightful, the question of whether it is history still remains.

A number of talented young Indians are beginning to emerge from the nation's graduate and professional schools—including law schools —with sophisticated critical skills and an undiminished social and racial consciousness. They have experienced the defects of the white educational system—insofar as Indian history is concerned—on the way up. These individuals will eventually, I believe, contribute to the writing of the history of their people. I am particularly optimistic about the role to be played by Indian students of the law, for there is no better way to gain an understanding of Indian history than through the documents and theory of the law which so profoundly shaped the course of Indian-white relations.

The writing of Indian history by Indians has been provided with institutional bases by the creation of Red Studies programs in various universities, by the establishment of Indian-run colleges such as the Navajo Community College, and by the organization of the American Indian Historical Society, 1451 Masonic Avenue, San Francisco, California 94117. The society, nursed to a vigorous young adulthood by Rupert Costo and Jeannette Henry, publishes *The Indian Historian*, an outlet for the work of Indian historians and white supporters of the cause of Indian history. In 1970 the society published a survey of the treatment of American Indians in school textbooks under the title, *Textbooks and the American Indian*, with Costo serving as editor and Henry as writer. Later in the year, the society published under the title, *Indian Voices*, the proceedings of the first conference of Indian historians held at Princeton University in the fall of 1969. While not free from the propagandistic pressures and ethnic sensitivities engendered by a concern with the cause of a single ethnic group, the American Indian Historical Society can justly claim to be serving history as well as the Indian people. This claim will be more fully validated as the first flush of enthusiasm for the Indian point of view is supplemented in the long run by an increasingly objective and detailed analysis of the facts of Indian history by the growing body of Indian and white scholars now being trained in the universities of the country.

There are dangers in too specialized a concern with particular aspects of a larger general history, but the study of the American Indian is less subject to the dangers of overspecialization than of unconcern. The number of Indian groups is so vast, the historical record so confused, or biased, or difficult of access, the change of status and culture so rapid, the life of the Indian so inextricably mixed with the white man's presence and his goods that one needs to focus special attention upon the Indian in order to clarify his history. At the present time, that history is affected not only by ignorance of the record but by prejudices and myths inherited from earlier centuries over which new myths and prejudices have been superimposed. The sharp disagreements of historians over the meaning of the already revealed record illustrates the many problems in the field which remain to be solved. It may be that historians are constitutionally incapable of meeting the challenge posed by Indian history and that the task will be performed by anthropologists or by the Indians themselves. I am inclined to think that the job will be done by historians going over the written record with a more judicial attitude and with greater sensitivity to the implications of cultural differences than an earlier generation of historians has displayed. And prominent among those historians will Indians but as historians dedicated to the elucidation and elaboration of the past. *be anthropologists and Indians writing not as anthropologists or as*

SINCE THE PUBLICATION of the article here reprinted, many excellent works on the American Indian have been published. Two outstanding ones are Joseph G. Jorgensen's *The Sun Dance Religion: Power for the Powerless* (Chicago: University of Chicago Press, 1972) and Warren L. Cook's *Flood Tide of Empire: Spain and the Northwest, 1543–1819* (New Haven and London: Yale University Press, 1973). These two books strengthen the conviction expressed in the original article that the boundary between anthropology and history is an arbitrary one and that a good book dealing with the American Indian requires an author familiar with the sources and methods of both disciplines. Cook is a historian; Jorgensen an anthropologist. Each has exhaustively mined the primary sources bearing on his subject, skillfully analyzed the data, and stated new interpretations. In Cook's case, the data are primarily in written form, and Cook has dealt effectively with collections (and their custodians) all over the world. Jorgensen, on the other hand, has relied primarily on field work with living subjects—Shoshoni Indians—whose respect he earned by his concern for their dignity as well as by his respect for the truth. Cook's work is informed by a thorough understanding of anthropology and the native point of view, while Jorgensen's work carefully considers the historical evidence available. Cook's book can be classified as a history of exploration and European national rivalry, while Jorgensen's study is an anthropological treatise on the evolution of a redemptive movement—the Sun Dance—among certain reservation Indians. Yet both books illuminate the *history* of the American Indian.

Among the many solid works of traditional historical scholarship that have appeared in the last few years, often in the University of Oklahoma's Civilization of the American Indian Series, two examples may suffice: William E. Unrau's *The Kansa Indians: A History of the Wind People, 1673–1873* (Norman, 1971), and Arrell M. Gibson's *The Chickasaws* (Norman, 1971). Unrau's book was written in the face of discouraging advice that the Kansa story could probably never be told for lack of sufficient evidence. His solid research, however, uncovered the data needed to provide a coherent picture of the tragic history of that tribe.

In the literary field, perhaps the outstanding work to appear in recent years is Richard Slotkin's *Regeneration through Violence: The Mythology of the American Frontier, 1600–1860* (Middletown, Conn.: Wesleyan University Press, 1973). Inevitably the Indian occupies a central role in the mythology of the frontier, and Slotkin comes directly to grips with the white man's perception of him. Not only in its comprehensiveness but in its sophisticated analysis Slotkin's work is a worthy companion to the books of Henry Nash Smith and Roy Harvey Pearce. Less satisfactory as intellectual history is Bernard W. Sheehan's *Seeds of Extinction: Jeffersonian Philanthropy and the American Indian* (Chapel Hill: University of North Carolina Press, 1973), which does not materially improve upon the dissertation version discussed in the original article.

A word about the progress of native scholarship may be in order. In the 1960s a great effort was made, by such agencies as the Office of Economic Opportunity and the Duke Oral History Project, to encourage the creation of tribal histories told from the native point of view. The results of that effort are beginning to appear. One of the first products is *The Zunis: Self-portrayals by the Zuni People,* Alvina Quam, translator (Albuquerque: University of New Mexico Press, 1972). Another, based on interviews conducted by the American Indian Research Project at the University of South Dakota, is *To Be an Indian: An Oral History,* edited by Joseph H. Cash and Herbert T. Hoover (New York: Holt, Rinehart and Winston, Inc., 1971). Although valuable contributions, these books are still not history in the technical sense, but raw material for history. One continues to await the utilization of the oral history record in true Indian history.

The Indian best known to the American public, Vine Deloria, Jr., has continued his extensive writing despite the pressure of innumerable competing demands on his time and reputation. Much of his activity, as in the compilation of the book *Of Utmost Good Faith* (San Francisco: Straight Arrow Books, 1971), has sought to make available to Indians and others the texts of treaties and agreements between the United States and the Indian tribes. At the same time he has helped to initiate legal action to secure Indian rights guaranteed under those treaties and agreements. Deloria's latest, and most powerful, statement is the book *God Is Red* (New York: Grosset & Dunlap, 1973), a searching comparative study of white and red religious points of view. Deloria contrasts the white concern with time with the Indian concern with space, the white concern with dominating nature with the Indian concern with being a part of it, the white concern with history with the Indian concern with shared experience. He sees an ultimate reconciliation between the spiritual owner of the land—the Indian—and the political owner—the white man. Recent political events, such as the capture of Wounded Knee and the sacking of the BIA, are discussed in terms of the underlying moral positions of both whites and Indians. While others—both white and Indian—have hastily jumped on contemporary activist bandwagons, often at the expense of objectivity and perspective, Deloria has been able to keep himself free of too close an identification with either the establishment or the anti-establishment. Thus he has been able to maintain his integrity as a moral man and as a perceptive observer which, if one thinks about it, may serve as an appropriate definition of a historian.

The Fatal Confrontation: Early Native-White Relations on the Frontiers of Australia, New Guinea, and America— A Comparative Study

WILBUR R. JACOBS

The author is professor of history in the University of California, Santa Barbara.

MOST INVESTIGATORS who have given serious study to man in pre-history tell us that Stone Age peoples in many parts of the world evolved a culture that gave them a reasonably satisfying life largely governed by the ecology of their habitat. On the Pacific islands, in Australia, and in North America, although patterns of life varied, native cultures seem to have put little strain on the land and biota. The beliefs and institutions of native people encouraged them to live in balance with the natural resources. For example, there are few instances of native peoples killing off animals that were a part of their food supply. The Pacific islanders who lived in delicate balance with plant and animal life evolved a culture governed by specialized tropical and oceanic environments. To a degree, the same generalization can be applied to the aborigines of Australia and to many North American Indians. In fact, all three peoples, including the ancestors of the native people of Papua-New Guinea, possessed a remarkable knowledge of plants and animals in their habitat and generally lived a life that today's conservationists would praise very highly indeed.[1]

This study was made possible by research grants from the Huntington Library, the American Philosophical Society, the Committee on the International Exchange of Persons, and the Committee on Research, University of California, Santa Barbara.

When the virgin areas were "discovered" by Occidentals, however, there were fundamental transformations in the ecological balance of the land which were brought about by superior technology. The native people, in most instances, were pushed aside and their lands were utilized for missions, Sunday schools, mines, plantations, farms, and grazing land. Even well meaning missionaries, in seeking to convert the natives into a labor force, often destroyed the lands and culture of the people they sought to protect.

Of the native people who survived the onslaught of the aliens, few retained their lands or even a portion of them. Many natives were simply killed off by bullets and disease, but some survived to become black or brown-skinned Europeans. Fewer still maintained their ancient ways and somehow clung to their land. In a sense, the

---

1 Douglas L. Oliver in his *Pacific Islands* (3rd ed., New York, 1961), ix, 1–80, stresses the importance of ecological factors in shaping the cultures of native peoples of the Pacific islands, New Guinea, and Australia. Similarly, Alfred L. Kroeber. Frank G. Speck, John M. Cooper, and William H. Fenton have described Indian cultures that maintained an ecological balance with wilderness areas. Speck, for example, in *The Penobscot Man* (Philadelphia, 1940), 207 ff., analyzes the family hunting ground system of the northeastern Indians, a method of conserving beaver supply. Debate on Speck's theories and discussion of the impact of the fur trade on the northeastern Indians is in Rolf Knight, "A Re-examination of Hunting, Trapping, and Territoriality among the Northeastern Indians," in Anthony Leeds and Andrew P. Vayda, eds., *Man, Culture, and Animals* (Washington, D.C., 1965), 27–41. Calvin Martin, in an unpublished paper, "The Algonquin Family Hunting Territory Revisited" (University of California, Santa Barbara) shows that evidence in the *Jesuit Relations* supports Speck's theories on Indian conservationist techniques. Further discussion on this point is in Eleanor Leacock, "The Montagnais 'Hunting Territory' and the Fur Trade," *American Anthropological Association Memoir No. 78* (Beloit, Wisconsin, 1954), 24–40. The remarkable agricultural techniques of the Hurons who successfully maintained productive corn fields for a dozen years or more are analyzed in Conrad E. Heidenreich, "The Geography of Huronia in the First Half of the 17th Century" (Ph.D. dissertation, McMaster University, 1970), 267–273. Paleo Indians and other Paleo peoples have sometimes been portrayed as destructive. For instance, the controversial hypothesis of the Pleistocene "overkill" of huge Ice-Age mammals by certain Paleo Indians some 12,000 years ago is examined from several sides by paleontologists, archaeologists, and ecologists in *Pleistocene Extinction: The Search for a Cause* (New Haven, Conn., 1967), 75 ff. The question of "overkill or overchill" is still unresolved. The controversy concerning the Indian and other native people as practitioners of burning (and thereby destroyers of flora and fauna) is discussed in Carl Sauer, *Land and Life* (Berkeley, 1965), 189–191. Sauer, discussing the matter in a letter to me of January 28, 1971, writes: "I think the case is pretty well made for man, and especially the Indians as practicers of burning. So the longer the aborigines and successors were around the bigger the grasslands and the more open the woodlands, the greater the number and diversity of . . . flowering, palatable plants. On balance this meant that there was more food than in fire free tracts. A forest has little food except at the tree tops and along the openings. Indian burning did change faunal composition but increased productivity of food of plant and animal."

real test of survival was possession of the land. Next to outright extermination the best technique for destroying natives was dispossessing them of their land. Land for the aborigines was all important
because it was a spiritual ingredient of their culture; it determined
their social groupings and status; and, finally, it was the source of
their livelihood. Thus, if there is a probable test for the survival of a
native people it is found in the answer to the question: how much of
their land have they retained after the alien invasion?[2]

The three widely-separated native people that are being compared
here, the American Indians, the Australian aborigines, and the natives
of New Guinea, exhibit striking similarities. All of them had lived for
centuries isolated from both western and oriental civilizations. Although North American Indians had copper ornaments, all groups
lived in what is called the Stone Age in a social world of clans, tribes,
and tribelets, many of them part of larger cultural groups loosely
related by ancestral and linguistic ties. All used wooden and stone
tools and weapons, and all constructed artifacts for a variety of religious, civic, and utilitarian purposes. All lived in a world of sorcery and
medicine men. In their societies, the men mainly occupied themselves
with hunting, and in making weapons, tools, and shelters, and in some
cases gardening, while women were generally concerned with child
care, gathering and preparing food, and often in making mats and
baskets.

The history of these people is primarily known to us through the
records of explorers, missionaries, government agents, and settlers.
All express the white man's point of view and are reflected in our
histories.[3] Historical materials are, of course, supplemented by modern
anthropological studies.[4] All these people had early relations with

---

2 See Douglas Oliver's perceptive essay on "The Dispossessed" in *The Pacific Islands*,
157–173.

3 Edward H. Spicer, in *Cycles of Conquest: The Impact of Spain, Mexico, and the
United States on the Indians of the Southwest*, 1533–1960 (Tucson, 1962), 581–582, discusses, for example, H.H. Bancroft's idea that "savages cannot be civilized under the
tuition of superior races," a point of view found in the sources Bancroft used.

4 The literature published by anthropologists on these native peoples is immense. A
selection of the main publications consulted for this paper includes A. L. Kroeber's
superb volume, *Anthropology, Race, Language, Culture, Psychology, Prehistory* (New
York, 1948), which digests a large mass of data published before 1948. The best work on
native Australians is A.P. Elkin's classic, *The Australian Aborigines: How to Understand Them* (3rd ed., Sydney, 1954). This is supplemented by a series of research studies
by Elkin's former students and admirers, *Aboriginal Man in Australia, Essays in Honour
of Emeritus Professor A. P. Elkin*, edited by Ronald M. Berndt and Catherine H. Berndt

Europeans, especially English-speaking Europeans. The Indians of North America, it will be recalled, had their frontiers invaded by waves of Spaniards, Dutch, French, Swedes, and English in the seventeenth and eighteenth centuries, and by Russians, Canadians, and Americans in the nineteenth century. Australia was visited by many European explorers and by Captain James Cook,[5] but the real invasion came when an English penal colony was planted there in

---

(Sydney, 1965), and an excellent paperback by R. M. and C. H. Berndt, *The First Australians* (Sydney, 1969). *The Australian Aborigines*, a short illustrated volume published by the Department of Territories (Sydney, 1967), tends to give a favorable coloration to government policies. D. J. Mulvaney, ed., "Australian Archaeology, A Guide to Field Techniques," *Australian Institute of Aboriginal Studies Manual No. 4* (Canberra, 1969), 119–130, has a classification of aboriginal stone implements. Mulvaney's comprehensive *Ancient Peoples and Places, the Prehistory of Australia* (London, 1969) shows aboriginal life to be in technological change. A basic research tool is Felix M. Keesing's comprehensive *Culture Change, An Analysis and Bibliography of Anthropological Sources to 1952* (Stanford, 1953).

Felix M. Keesing's comprehensive *Culture Change, An Analysis and Bibliography of Anthropological Sources to 1952* (Stanford, 1953).

One of the best modern studies on the native people of New Guinea is by a political scientist, C. D. Rowley, whose *The New Guinea Villager* (Melbourne, 1965) is based upon firsthand experience. *Pigs for the Ancestors: Ritual in the Ecology of a New Guinea People*, by Roy A. Rappaport (New Haven, 1967), is a technical study showing how close the ritual cycle of native people in Tsembaga governed their adjustment to their environment (see especially pp. 224–242). The Tsembaga people keep four kinds of animals: pigs, chickens, dogs, and dassowaries; the tame birds are captured as chicks and provide meat and feathers. Other useful volumes on the New Guinea villagers are: H. Ian Hogbin, *Transformation Scene: The Changing Culture of a New Guinea Village* (London, 1951); Gavin Souter, *New Guinea: The Last Unknown* (London, 1963); Brian Essai, *Papua and New Guinea: A Contemporary Survey* (London, 1961); and *Studies in New Guinea Land Tenure: Three Papers*, by Ian Hogbin and Peter Lawrence (Sydney, 1967). An excellent survey of the island and its native people by two geographers is *New Guinea: The Territory and Its People*, by D. A. M. Lea and P. G. Irwin (Melbourne, 1967).

Basic for the study of the North American Indians are Frederick Webb Hodge, ed., *Handbook of the American Indian North of Mexico* (2 vols., Washington, D.C. 1907, 1910); Hodge, ed., *Handbook of Indians of Canada* (Ottawa, 1913); A. L. Kroeber, *Handbook of the Indians of California* (Washington, 1925); Kroeber, *Cultural and Natural Areas of Native North America* (Berkeley, 1939); John R. Swanton, *Indian Tribes of North America* (Washington, 1953); and S. F. Cook's statistical studies on *The Conflict between the California Indian and White Civilization* (4 vols., Berkeley, 1943), supplemented by the excellent bibliographical notes in Wendell H. Oswalt, *This Land Was Theirs: A Study of the North American Indian* (New York, 1966). William Brandon's *The American Heritage Book of Indians* (New York, 1961) is a readable history of the Indians brilliantly incorporating a large mass of anthropological data.

5 J. C. Beaglehole, ed., *The Journals of Captain James Cook on His Voyages of Discovery, The Voyage of the Endeavor* (Cambridge, England, 1955), 508, includes a passage from a letter written by Cook in 1771 which gives a kind of noble savage image of mainland Australian aborigines: "These people may truly be said to be in the pure state of Nature, and may appear to some to be the most wretched upon the Earth: but in reality they are far more happier than . . . we Europeans, [since,] being wholly unacquinted [sic] . . . with the superfluous . . . necessary Conveniencies so much sought after in Europe[,] they are happy in not knowing the use of them. . . ." Cook and other writers stressed that the aborigines seemed happy living on only the bare necessities, yet Europeans were unhappy. There was an undercurrent of dissatisfaction with civilization

1788.[6] The large island of New Guinea was contacted by Portuguese, Spanish, and Dutch explorers in the early 1700s and by Captain James Cook in 1770.[7] Europeans established small settlements on the coasts of New Guinea in the early 1800s.

The native populations of the three areas had strong religious, social, and economic ties with their lands and all resisted European occupation. Generally, territorial rights of specific native groups were respected by other natives in spite of tribal rivalries and conflicts. Identification with specific areas of land was almost always characterized by sacred landmarks and placenames.[8] These native people lived according to what the conservationist Aldo Leopold has called a *land ethic*. Their sacred rituals, mythology, and religious songs were generally tied to the rhythm of the seasons, the growth of plants and animals, and the ancestral deities who created the world. Groups of natives usually claimed descent from a particular totem, perhaps part animal and part human. Totemism, a concept of life unifying all living things in nature with man as a central figure, had no counterpart in European thought and was seldom understood by the whites who first contacted native people.[9] The aboriginal's respect for the land emerges from his close spiritual ties with nature. Despite the

---

because it had abandoned nature. Alan Moorehead in his perceptive book, *The Fatal Impact, An Account of the Invasion of the South Pacific,* 1767–1840 (Ringwood, Victoria, Australia, 1966), 150–151, comments on this attitude of certain Pacific explorers.

[6] C. M. H. Clark, ed., *Select Documents in Australian History, 1788-1850* (Sydney, 1969), 43 ff.

[7] Donald Craigie Gordon, *The Australian Frontier in New Guinea, 1870–1885* (New York, 1951), 19–42, summarizes activities of first explorers in New Guinea. See also Andrew Sharp, *The Discovery of Australia* (London, 1963), 21 ff.

[8] A. P. Elkin's chapter, "The Land and the Aborigines," in his *The Australian Aborigines,* 24–48; essay on aboriginal land rights dated Nov. 15, 1839, possibly written by John D. Lang (1799–1878), clergyman and early anthropologist, in manuscript volume labeled "Aborigines," A 610, Mitchell Library, Sydney; *Indian Place Names, Their Origin, Evolution, and Meaning,* by John Rydjord (Norman, Oklahoma, 1968); Erwin G. Gudde, *California Placenames: The Origin and Etymology of Current Geographical Names* (2nd ed., Berkeley, 1960), and the linguistic and ethnographic criticism of this book by William Bright in the *American Journal of Folklore,* LXXV (1962), 78–82; A. L. Kroeber, *California Placenames of Indian Origin* (Berkeley, 1916), diagram 2; "Religious Beliefs and Change of Land Rights," in Hogbin and Lawrence, *Studies in New Guinea Land Tenure,* 117.

[9] Elkin, *The Australia Aborigines,* 132–155; R. M. and C. H. Berndt, *The First Australians,* 74–78; Kroeber, *Anthropology,* 396; William N. Fenton, "The Iroquois in History," paper read at the Wenner-Gren Symposium, Burg Wartenstein, Austria, August 7–14, 1967; Hodge, *Handbook of the American Indian,* part II, 787–795. New Guinea natives' shamanism, magic, and animistic ritual is described in Rappaport, *Pigs for Ancestors,* especially "Pigs, Eels, and Fertility," 210–213.

many variations of Indian, aboriginal, and native New Guinea religious myths and totemism, all appear to have much in common.
The lives these native people led, judged by our standards, were
brutal and hard. Yet they succeeded in adapting themselves to their
environment and lived in relative harmony with their natural sur-
roundings. They even had certain types of population control.[10]
Generations lived and died, seemingly without population explosions
or widespread starvation.

Much of New Guinea, especially the western part called West Irian
(now part of Indonesia), is practically the same as it was thousands
of years ago. Village life is almost unchanged. Before the arrival of
Europeans these dark-skinned, wooly-haired people (the Papuan and
Melanesian natives differ in stature, hair-texture, and features from
each other) had established a subsistence village life based upon
gardening, hunting, and fishing. Their domestic animals were the
dog, the pig, and the chicken, while staple foods were yams, bananas,
and the sago palm. Villages were isolated from each other by pre-
cipitous mountains, swamplands, or jungles. Feuding tribes, having
no common bond of language, fought for grisly trophies of human
heads and flesh. Sorcery, exchange of food and gifts, reciprocal "pay-
back" justice, feasts, dances, and condolence ceremonies for the dead
are as familiar to the student of the North American Indian as to the
student of the Australian aborigines.[11] The New Guinea natives, like
all other indigenous people of tropical countries, suffer from a variety
of diseases that limit population growth. Half of the infants born in
the Sepik River interior villages where I visited last year die before

---

10 Benjamin Franklin described Iroquois population control in this way: "The number
of savages generally does not increase in North America. Those living near the Europeans
steadily diminish in numbers and strength. The two sexes are of a cold nature, for the
men find that the women refuse to sleep with them as soon as they become pregnant.
For they believe that makes childbirth difficult. Further, they suckle their children for
two and a half or three full years and for the whole time they refrain from sleeping
with men." Leonard W. Labaree, ed., The Papers of Benjamin Franklin (New Haven,
1969), XIII, 351. For a modern appraisal of this method of limiting population growth,
see Christopher Tietze, "The Effect of Breastfeeding on the Rate of Conception," Proceedings of the International Population Conference (New York, 1961), II, 129–136.
Among Dr. Tietze's conclusions are: "Since . . . breastfeeding tends to prolong the in-
terval between pregnancies, it seems worthwhile to evaluate it as a method of child
spacing" (p. 133).

11 Rowley, The New Guinea Villager, 32–52; P. Biskup, B. Jinks, and H. Nelson, A
Short History of New Guinea (Sydney, 1968), 1–28. The variety of modern primitive life
is described by a former patrol officer, J. P. Sinclair, in his Behind the Ranges, Patrolling
New Guinea (Melbourne, 1966).

their first birthday. Malaria, a repulsive infection called "grilli" that flakes the skin, and hookworm are age-old enemies, but the special gifts of transient Europeans and Orientals, leprosy, tuberculosis, and venereal disease, have also taken their toll.[12] Voracious clouds of night-flying mosquitoes force individual natives to crawl into huge straw stockings to escape being almost eaten alive. Yet everywhere in Papua–New Guinea the natives appear to live today in reasonable prosperity on their own lands. Mountain villagers own coffee plantations that encircle their gardens and straw-roofed matted buildings. The river and jungle villages in rows of homes, many with second story apartments, are owned by the tribes which have lived there for centuries. The garden-sorcerer, who produces yams as huge as a man, gardens in a plot used by his ancestors for generations.[13]

Why, we may ask, have the natives of New Guinea been allowed to keep their land when the Australian aborigines and the American Indians were dispossessed? Why is the native population of Papua-New Guinea nearly two million while the non-indigenous people (Europeans, Chinese, and others) number only twenty-five thousand? A seasoned British explorer of 1890 put the question this way: "Will he [the New Guinea native] too disappear before the impact of the white race, like the Tasmanian and the Australian aboriginals have done? I think not," the explorer argued, because "the house-building, horticultural Papuan differs as much from the Australian nomad as the Malay or the Samoan differ from the feebler races they dispossessed."[14] Almost immediately the Europeans realized that they could not evict the New Guinea natives. They were firmly entrenched in their villages, fighting with terrible ferocity when attacked or threatened. Because of the complexity and variety of their language patterns and the diversity of local cultures, no friendly tribe or village could easily be used to conquer others or to aid whites in seizing control of

---

12 The specific new diseases that caused depopulation among Pacific islanders and Australian aborigines after contacts with Europeans are discussed in Felix M. Keesing, *The South Seas in the Modern World* (New York, 1941), 57 ff., 367; Kroeber, *Anthropology*, 182 ff. Kroeber makes the point that epidemics, once so deadly to islanders and American Indians, are reduced to the level of mild virulence after a generation or two. Edward Spicer stresses a cycle theory of the conquest and withdrawal of Europeans which may leave behind newly-invigorated native societies much enriched by cultural exchange. Spicer, *Cycles of Conquest*, 568.

13 Rowley, *The New Guinea Villager*, 115.

14 Theodore F. Bevan, *Toil, Travel, and Discovery in British Guinea* (London, 1890), 276.

the interior. The harsh climate, the virulent jungle diseases, the forbidding swamps, impenetrable jungles, and steep mountain cliffs gave villagers additional protection. Certainly there was no question of native claims to ownership of the land. Villagers clearly defined their systems of land tenure and garden plots (somewhat similar to those of the Iroquois) through a complex mixture of village, family (descent groups), and individual rights which allowed householders the exclusive privilege of cultivating certain allotments.[15]

Although the Dutch, Germans, British, and, later, the Australians acquired limited areas of land for trade and plantations near white settlements, there was never a concerted attempt to take over native land rights. The history of Papua-New Guinea reveals that soon after their 1883 occupation of Papua, the southeastern part of the island, the British decided to prevent dispossession of the natives. The special commissioner's report on New Guinea of 1886-1887 states, for example, that "the land question is no doubt the cardinal one upon which almost everything connected with British policy will turn."[16] Within two years the "protectorate" administration, as it called itself, published regulations clearly outlining basic rules governing native-white relations. Whites were not permitted to purchase land or to have any interest in land obtained from native people, who, in turn, were forbidden to sell to whites. Only the imperial government could negotiate purchases. This discreet policy, along with regulations prohibiting the sale of arms and intoxicants to natives or exploitation of the natives as laborers, helped to prevent native explosions of outrage caused by occasional white abuses. An ordinance of 1888, for example, prohibited "removal" of natives from their own district except "for purposes of education or the advancement of religious teaching."[17]

When the British imperial government formally annexed Papua by a proclamation read at Port Moresby in 1888, some decades after the beginning of British penetration of the area, the Germans had already established themselves in the area immediately to the north, and the

---

15 Hogbin and Lawrence, *Studies in New Guinea Land Tenure*, xiii, 32–33, 100–134.

16 Statement by John Douglas, "Her Majesty's Special Commissioner to New Guinea," Dec. 31, 1886, *British New Guinea, Report for the Year 1886* (Victoria, 1887), 8. A collection of early British reports on the protectorate is preserved in the New Guinea History Collection, Library of the University of Papua-New Guinea, Port Moresby.

17 *British New Guinea Annual Report, Her Majesty's Administrator of Government from 4th of September, 1888, to 30th June 1889* (Melbourne, Victoria, 1890), 6.

western part of the island had been annexed by the Dutch as Nether-lands New Guinea. The native people on the coast and on neighbor-ing islands had been exposed earlier to Moslem and European slave recruiters, and to a variety of Christian missionaries, Catholic, Angli-can, Lutheran, and Methodist. A large number of the islanders had served as laborers in Queensland or on German Samoa plantations and had brought back bitter reports of exploitation. In the year 1883 there were more than thirty ships recruiting native labor on the shores of New Guinea.[18]

However, the islanders fought back. Papuan ferocity in combat was not easily forgotten. Missionaries suffered incredible hardships. A British commentator in 1886 complained that the native response to "the message of Christ" was that of "a savage race of inhuman mur-derers."[19] In German New Guinea, white control went no further than the fringes of settlement. Newspaper files at the library of the University of Papua-New Guinea show the remarkable slowness of the penetration of European government into the wilderness even after Australian authority was extended over the eastern part of the island in 1914. As late as 1931 a Port Moresby newspaper complained that "the remote tribes . . . have hardly been under [European] influence at all."[20] Handicapped by the tropical climate, rugged terrain, and the bewildering complexity of native languages, patrol officers found they had another foe, sorcery, which was, as one visitor put it, "the very air of Papua."[21] When native officers took the field, they sometimes hailed sorcerers before white magistrates for such bizarre offenses as "causing rain to fall at an inopportune time." In a land where there are some-times two hundred inches of rain a year, the rainmaker could be a formidable villain.[22]

The remarkable perserverance until today of sorcery and such cus-toms as "pay-back" justice indicates how slow the white man's civili-zation has been in penetrating New Guinea. These people have never

---

18 Biskup *et al.*, *A Short History of New Guinea*, 25. This labor trade, sometimes called "the blackbirding trade," often differed little in practice from slaving. Rowley, *The New Guinea Villager*, 58.

19 *British New Guinea Report for the Year 1886*, pp. 8–9.

20 *Papuan Courier*, June 16, 1931.

21 *Ibid.* Perceptive comments on native sorcery are in Beatrice Grimshaw, *The New Guinea* (Philadelphia, 1911), 200; Hogbin, *Transformation Scene: The Changing Culture of a New Guinea Village*, 136, 142–147, 222–226.

22 Lea and Irwin, *New Guinea: The Territory and Its People*, 18–19, chart rainfall up to 250 inches per year in parts of New Guinea and New Britain.

really been conquered by Europeans. They have never been deprived of their lands by an encompassing frontier of white settlement. There has been native acculturation but without dominance or assimilation. Like many of the American Indians and many Australian aborigines, some New Guineans have accepted the white man's money, his religion, his items of dress, and other tangibles of civilization, but they have kept their old customs and rituals. Like some of the Indians and Australian aborigines, they resisted spiritual domination by the white man. The native people in New Guinea, however, seem to have been moderately successful in maintaining their old ways and a larger degree of self-determination because they still control the ownership of the great mass of land. The original British occupation of the area around the large native village at Port Moresby in 1873 did not go far beyond the double rows of native houses and rows of swaying coconut palms where flourished an extensive trade in pottery, garden products, and sago palm flour.[23]

Today, some hundred years later, Port Moresby is much changed, but the center of the city still has its large native market. It is in this city that the native people have a strong voice in self-government through an elected legislative council.[24]

The history of early native-white contacts on the frontiers of Papua-New Guinea, then, is different from that of North America or Australia largely because the American Indians and the Australian aborigines were driven from their lands, especially in areas of rich soil where climate sustained lush vegetation. When the native peoples were overrun by advancing white frontiers, as in Australia and North America or on Pacific islands such as New Zealand, investigators have discerned three distinct periods in the acculturation of tribes or groups of aborigines. In the first stage of white contact, friendly relations often developed because of native hospitality and presents offered by the whites. As whites encroached upon native lands, early friendship soured and within decades native resentment grew. Finally, warfare resulted in

---

23 The gradual changes of the "salubrius" native village of 800 native people located at the site of Port Moresby is described in *Australasia*, by Élisée Reclus, edited by A. H. Keane (London [1889]), 313–314.

24 Brian Essai, *Papua and New Guinea: A Contemporary Survey* (Melbourne, 1961), 237–238; Albert Maori Kiki, *Kiki, Ten Thousand Years in a Lifetime, A New Guinea Autobiography* (Melbourne, 1968), 161–187, gives the viewpoint of an elected leader of the New Guinea native people. See also John Wilkes, ed., *New Guinea . . . Future Indefinite?* (Sydney, 1968), 139–167.

defeat of the natives and bewildered loss of respect for their own culture.[25]

In the second period, an era of depopulation and despondence that sometimes covered several decades or even a half century, the native people often developed a scorn for many of their own customs. This was usually a time when they suffered from the onslaught of smallpox, tuberculosis, venereal disease, and alcoholism. After portions of their lands and sacred places had been occupied by whites, they were often left without leadership. Finally, there was a stage that the noted Australian anthropologist, A. P. Elkin, calls an era of contra-acculturation.[26] In this period the natives tended to revive their culture in modified form with renewed appreciation of their own arts, crafts, and rituals. If native societies reached this third stage, as the Seneca Indians did with the rise of the prophet Handsome Lake, they usually survived as a people with their own cultural heritage. Otherwise they perished or were assimilated by the whites.

The Seneca took nearly two hundred years to complete this cycle of acculturation. Like the Maoris of New Zealand, who experienced a similar cycle in their confrontations with whites, the Seneca were fierce warriors who had at first held Europeans at bay. The Seneca, in fact, prospered after their initial contacts with the Dutch, French, and British in the seventeenth century. Despite the disappearance of fur bearing animals from their country in western New York, they prof-

---

25 A. P. Elkin has criticized the missionaries who had good intentions but nevertheless were destructive pioneers of white civilization in breaking down native cultures without making replacement. His strictures are in *The Australian Aborigines*, 29, 44, 156–162 ff., and are echoed in A. Grenfell Price, *White Settlers and Native Peoples . . .* (Melbourne, 1949), 194. Missions appear to have created a cycle of destruction that is typically uniform among both the Australian aboriginals and the California Indians causing the virtual disappearance of full-blood native people within fifty years. Price, *White Settlers and Native People*, 194–195, and Cook, *The Conflict Between the California Indian and White Civilization: The Indian Versus the Spanish Mission*, 3–12, 15, 113–128.

Elkin's discussion of "Phases in Aboriginal-European Contact" is in *The Australian Aborigines*, 321–328, and in a slightly revised form in Price, *White Settlers and Native People*, 196. A similar discussion is in Felix M. Keesing, *The South Seas in the Modern World* (New York, 1941), 79–80. Keesing's study of *The Menomini Indians of Wisconsin: A Study of Three Centuries of Cultural Contact and Change* (Philadelphia, 1939) reveals a recognizable tribal identity among these Indians, but only fragments of their aboriginal culture survived. The Senecas were relatively successful in preserving elements of their culture according to Anthony F. C. Wallace in his *The Death and Rebirth of the Seneca* (New York, 1969), 303–337.

26 Elkin, "The Reaction of Primitive Races to the White Man's Culture," *Hibbert Journal*, XXXV (1937), 537–545, cited in Price, *White Settlers and Native People*, 196, 225.

ited from their role as middlemen in the fur trade between the Anglo-Dutch traders at Albany and the Indians of the Great Lakes. They sustained themselves with a diet based upon maize, squash, beans, and nuts, and protected themselves by "the Great Binding Law" or Iroquois "constitution" which bound the Seneca to the Five Nations confederacy.[27]

In their prime during the 1750s, the Seneca, with their fellow-Iroquois, maintained almost a balance of power between France and England.[28] But when the eighteenth-century wars of the forest ended, they lost much of their land. After the American Revolution, they were forced into a reservation life that has been called "slums in the wilderness." The 1799 vision of Handsome Lake, a reformed drunkard and Seneca chief, marked the beginning of a new era for his people, a renaissance in Iroquois technology, a rehabilitation of the Iroquois cultural health, and the beginning of the Longhouse or Handsome Lake Church.[29]

Not all Indian prophets had the success of Handsome Lake. A Delaware prophet of the 1750s had his message taken over by an Ottawa chief, Pontiac, who unsuccessfully led northeastern tribes in one of the last great wars of the forest. These religious movements, which appeared among the plains tribes in the nineteenth century, have sometimes been called "cults of despair." Across the Pacific, full-blood and half-caste Australian aborigines attempted to revive the rites and beliefs of their ancestors.[30]

Most of the aboriginals of North America and Australia have worked out a partial assimilation on their own as a result of living within a conquered territory. The Navajo, who stem from the Atha-

---

27 William N. Fenton, ed., *Parker on the Iroquois, Iroquois Uses of Maize and Other Food Plants, The Code of Handsome Lake, the Seneca Prophet, the Constitution of the Five Nations* (Syracuse, New York, 1968), Introduction, pages 25–47; Book One, pages 5–113; Book Three, pages 7–132.

28 Wilbur R. Jacobs, *Wilderness Politics and Indian Gifts, The Northern Colonial Frontier* (Lincoln, Neb., 1966), 5, 159 ff. An excellent documented account of the dispossession of Iroquois tribal communities is in Georgiana C. Nammack, *Fraud, Politics and the Dispossession of the Indians, The Iroquois Land Frontier in the Colonial Period* (Norman, Oklahoma, 1969), 22–106.

29 Fenton, ed., *Parker on the Iroquois*, Book Two, pages 5–138; Wallace, *The Death and Rebirth of the Seneca*, 239 ff.

30 Elkin, *The Australian Aborigines*, 328–338. For the relationship between the Delaware Prophet and Pontiac, mentioned above, see Wilbur R. Jacobs, "Was the Pontiac Uprising a Conspiracy?" *Ohio Archaeological and Historical Society Quarterly*, LIX (1950), 26–37.

pascan Apache, borrowed weaving and planting of corn from the Pueblo tribes, and later silversmithing and sheepherding from the Spaniards. By skillfully adapting these to the arid land left them by the whites, they have increased in population and today are a proud, largely self-sustaining people who have strongly resisted assimilation into white society.[31]

The histories of the Seneca and the Navajo are exceptional in the overall story of Indian-white confrontations on America's frontiers. Many tribes were simply unable to withstand the powerful impact of white frontiers of exploration and settlement. In both Australia and America there was a disintegration of native societies directly adjacent to white settlements, especially in areas where there had been a high native population density.

The highest concentration of native population in both North America and Australia was in areas of moderate rainfall and lush vegetation along coasts and islands of both continents. As A. L. Kroeber repeatedly emphasized, rainfall variations and climatic conditions had a significant influence on the growth of native cultures and population densities. The harvesting of maize by the eastern Indians and the gathering of acorns by the California Indians contributed to the density of Indian population.[32]

Among the coastal Indians of North America and aborigines of Australia hunting and living areas were usually well defined. These were the areas quickly penetrated by land-hungry whites because of the fertility of the soil and the agreeable climatic conditions that were similar to those in Europe.

The advance of the white frontiers of settlement was generally conditioned by the same factors that originally determined native population patterns and the character of native hunting, harvesting, and food gathering areas. In great arid regions such as the Aranda Plain of central Australia, a tribal hunting and food gathering territory might embrace 25,000 square miles.[33] Whites generally avoided such areas except for periodic mining booms. Natives of the interior scattered so thinly throughout a large desert zone were not quickly conquered

---

31 Kroeber, *Anthropology*, 431. Kroeber makes the interesting point that, if by a miracle a major Indian tribe had conquered the whites, our culture would be perhaps only slightly modified (p. 430).

32 Kroeber, *Cultural and Natural Areas of Native North America*, 46, 52, 206–228.

33 Australian Department of Territories, *The Australian Aborigines* (Sydney, 1967), 6.

or assimilated. Indeed, a few remain wild and free today. At the time of discovery, there were some 300,000 aborigines in Australia, about one individual for every ten square miles.[34] Before the coming of the whites there were, according to a number of authorities, about one million Indians in what is now the United States, about one for every two to three square miles.[35]

Despite the superior fighting qualities of the Indians and their larger numbers, they were not able to hold off the advancing frontier after the colonial period, and, had they not had the alliance of the French fur-trading interests, it is doubtful if the Anglo-American westward movement would have been held at the Appalachians after the early 1750s.[36] In Australia, a small population of white settlers and convict laborers easily overran in a few decades the best areas occupied by the aborigines on the southeastern shore of Australia and the large island of Tasmania. New Guinea, by contrast a land of rugged terrain and lush tropical vegetation, supported a native population said to be as high as 500 per square mile in some areas, a strong barrier to whites who at first barely held their own on the fringes of the island.[37]

The Australian aborigines who were so easily dispossessed and conquered resembled in many respects the California Indians. These tribesmen, it will be recalled, were easily forced into the Spanish mission system and later left to fend for themselves after the secularization of mission lands and the occupation of California by the advancing

---

34 *Ibid.*, 3.

35 By 1900 the native Indian population had dwindled to some 250,000. Estimates of the modern Indian population range from 450,000 to 550,000. The Indian population is expected to go above 700,000 by 1975 according to William Brandon in his *The American Heritage Book of Indians*, 360. The current debate on Indian population estimates is highlighted by Henry F. Dobyns's statistical study, "Estimating Aboriginal American Population, An Appraisal of Techniques with a New Hemisphere Estimate" *Current Anthropology*, VII (1966), 395–449. Dobyns's startling conclusion is that "the New World was inhabited by approximately 90,000,000 persons immediately prior to discovery." He estimates the Indian population of North America at 9,800,000! (pp. 415–416). If Dobyns's estimates are valid (and they are carefully evaluated by qualified scholars who offer critiques in accompanying pages in the article), Europe (with a population of some 100,000,000) may well be considered an invader of new lands with native peoples who had almost the same population. Dobyns believes that epidemic diseases caused the widespread Indian depopulation which occurred soon after white contacts (pp. 412 ff). See also note 87.

36 Indians lost their importance as a balance of power after 1763. W. R. Jacobs, "British-Colonial Attitudes and Policies Toward the Indian in the American Colonies," in H. H. Peckham and Charles Gipson, eds., *Attitudes of the Colonial Powers Toward the Indian* (Salt Lake City, 1969), 81–106.

37 Biskup *et al, A Short History of New Guinea*, 8, a Chimbu area estimate.

American frontier.[38] When A. L. Kroeber in 1954 wrote a paper on "The Nature of Land-Holding Groups in Aboriginal California" in connection with a California Indian land claims case, he made a brilliant summary of tribal use of the land.[39] These Indians were particularly vulnerable to exploitation. Living by hunting, fishing, and acorn and root gathering, they had no art except basketry, no elaborate dances, no cultivated gardens or fields of maize. They lived in rude huts in small communities, and, though often naked, sometimes had rush aprons or skin robes. To the Europeans, their open brush lands might appear useless, but they yielded rabbits, birds, and other animals for food. Forest stands sheltered browsing deer. Each tract, well defined in area, was a source of food to be harvested. Many tribelets moved from area to area in season, fishing in winter and spring, hunting during summer and fall. Like the aborigines of Australia, they did not tame and breed animals except the dog. Acorns were a primary food, and there was a variety of other wild foods: fruits, berries, seeds, and fleshy root stalks.[40]

These tribelets resembled the sub-tribes of Australian aborigines, small food gathering groups called *hordes*. Unlike the Indians, the aborigines had no villages; they were semi-nomadic hunters, collectors, and fishermen who moved across the land. The men stalked the kangaroo or emu or speared fish. The women collected wild fruits, yams, nuts, seeds, grubs, stems, and roots.[41] Each aboriginal horde's hunting and living territory was clearly defined and respected by other groups. Yet, as one Australian pioneer opined, such people were "strolling savages" without a particular home or habitation.[42]

Other Australian pioneers questioned this approach which tended

---

38 The deplorable condition of many of the California Indians after American occupation is described in *The Indians of Southern California in 1852: The B. D. Wilson Report and a Selection of Contemporary Comment*, edited by John W. Caughey (San Marino, Calif., 1952). See also Cook, *The Conflict between the California Indian and White Civilization, The American Invasion, 1848–1870*, pp. 5–95.

39 Kroeber, "The Nature of Land-Holding Groups in Aboriginal California," in *Aboriginal California: Three Studies in Cultural History* (Berkeley, Calif., 1963), 81–120.

40 *Ibid.*; William Brandon, "The California Indian World," *The Indian Historian*, II (Summer, 1969), 4–7.

41 Elkin, *The Australian Aborigines*, 1–23.

42 "I confess myself at a loss to comprehend how a few strolling savages, entirely ignorant . . . [and] averse to cultivating the land[,] . . . may be said to possess a small portion of it today by erecting their crude huts, [since they] will abandon it tomorrow. . . ." Diary of Mary Thomas, p. 185, quoted in Ralph M. Hague, typescript MS,

to justify the dispossession of nomadic people. In 1839 a sympathetic Australian defended the natives and their right to the land:

In short every tribe has its own district & boundaries [and these] are well known to the natives generally; and within that district all of the wild animals are considered as the property of the tribe ranging on its whole extent [, just] as the flocks of sheep and herds of cattle that have been introduced by adventurous Europeans . . . are held by European law & usage the property of the respective owners. In fact as the country is occupied chiefly for pastoral purposes the differences between the aboriginal and European ideas of property and the soil is more imaginary than real.[43]

The author of this interesting comparison between aborigines and Australian settlers, who was probably a Presbyterian clergyman and amateur anthropologist,[44] went on to compare the kangaroos and the wild cattle. "The only difference being," he stated, "that the former are not branded with a particular mark like the latter, & are somewhat wilder and more difficult to catch." Furthermore, he claimed, "particular districts are not merely the property of particular tribes, particular sections of these districts are universally recognized by the natives as the property of individual members of the tribes." Finally, he pointed out a factor of great importance: "the infinity of the natives' names of places, all of which are descriptive & appropriate[,] is of itself prima facie evidence of their having strong ideas of property and the soil."[45]

There were few other whites who wanted to consider property rights of the aborigines in pioneer Australia. Most clergymen, and even the various "protectors" of the aborigines, usually former preachers who were appointed by the government to round up native tribes and to move them to a new area, had a condescending, fatalistic attitude toward the natives.[46] In justification of the occupation of Tasmanian

---

"The Law in South Australia, 1836–67," chap. 11, p. 3, State Library of South Australia, Archives Dept., Accession No. 1051.

43 [John D.] Lang, essay in manuscript volume labeled "Aborigines," A 610, Mitchell Library. A portion of the signature on this document is obscured.

44 *Ibid.* See also note 8.

45 Lang, "Aborigines," A 610, Mitchell Library.

46 See, for example, [George Augustus] "Robinson's Reports," on the Tasmanian Aborigines," A 612, pp. 76–77, Mitchell Library, Sydney; see especially the letter dated Sept. 9, 1829, from Robinson to Governor George Arthur, in which Robinson comments on "the mortality" that "has pervaded the whole aboriginal population." Robinson

lands, a prelude to complete extermination of the natives (after Lt. Governor George Arthur organized a manhunt across the island in 1830), one clergyman wrote, "it cannot be supposed that providence would desire any country to the occupancy of a few savages who make no further use of it than wandering from place to place when at the same time millions of human beings in other places are crowded upon one another without means of subsisting."[47]

Here, then, we have the two contrasting arguments on dispossession of native people, both made by English clergymen in Australia in the 1830s. Similar arguments were made by those who wished to dispossess the American Indians, as Wilcomb Washburn has pointed out in a learned article.[48] When Theodore Roosevelt wrote that "justice" was on the side of the pioneers because "this great continent could not have been kept as nothing but a game reserve for squalid savages,"[49] he echoed the opinions of such eminent figures in American history as John Winthrop, John Adams, Lewis Cass, John C. Calhoun, and Thomas Hart Benton who argued that a nomadic, primitive race must give way to a Christian, agricultural, civilized society.[50] Much of the justification rested upon Biblical quotations purporting to show that white people had prior rights to the land because they "used it according to the intentions of the creator."[51] The argument that nomadic hunters could be forced to alter their economy by an agricultural or

---

wrote that after contact with "white men" the aborigines were "imbibed [with] similar debauched habits and vicious propensities."

On the creation of the "protectorate" system by the British government in 1838–1842, see Box 3, "Aboriginal Protectorate," State Library of Victoria Archives, Melbourne. A "Chief Protector" was appointed with four assistant protectors, each officer to have a "district." He was to induce natives "to assume more settled habits of life . . . and watch over the rights and interests of the natives. . . ." These officers had duties somewhat similar to those of the Indian superintendents in the British colonies. See W. R. Jacobs, ed., *The Appalachian Indian Frontier, The Edmond Atkin Report and Plan of 1755* (Lincoln, Neb., 1967), xvi ff.

47 Comment by Thomas Henry Braim (1814–1891), Anglican clergyman of Hobart and Sydney in a handwritten essay, "The Aborigines," pp. 3–4, A 614, Mitchell Library.

48 Washburn, "The Moral and Legal Justifications for Dispossessing the Indians," in James M. Smith, ed., *Seventeenth-Century America: Essays in Colonial History* (Chapel Hill, 1959), 15–32.

49 Quoted in *ibid.*, 23.

50 See Albert K. Weinberg's well-documented chapter, "The Destined Use of the Soil," in *Manifest Destiny, A Study of Nationalist Expansionism in American History* (Baltimore, 1935), 72–99.

51 Statement by Senator Thomas H. Benton. Quoted in *ibid.*, 73.

pastoral people had first, though not systematically, been advanced by John Locke.[52]

The nomadic aborigines of Australia were also held in low esteem by almost all whites from the time of early exploration and settlement. Most Europeans shared the opinion of the seventeenth-century explorer William Dampier who described their "great bottle noses, pretty full lips, and wide mouths." "Their Eye-Lids," he said, "are always half closed, to keep the Flies out of their Eyes." These people, he said, "differ but little from Brutes," having no houses, domestic animals, fruits, or "skin garments."[53] Anthony Trollope's harsh judgment two centuries later is representative of the prevalent white attitude toward the natives: "Of the Australian black man we may certainly say that he has to go. That he should perish without unnecessary suffering should be the aim of all who are concerned in the matter." Trollope went so far as to write that should the "race" increase it "would be a curse rather than a blessing."[54] He reached this decision despite the remarkable "proficiency" of the children in school. The blacks, he tells us confidently, "are being exterminated by the footsteps of the advancing race."[55] The eminent Anglican clergyman of Australia in the early 1800s, the Rev. Samuel Marsden, held the blacks in such contempt that he felt they were not worth the missionary effort required for conversion. Indeed, their misery, he held, resulted from a special punishment inflicted upon them because of the sins of their ancestors in the Garden of Eden.[56] Marsden, though enthusiastic about missionary work among the Maoris in New Zealand, concluded that the Australian blacks "have no Reflections—they have no attachments, and they have no wants."[57]

The comments of Marsden, Trollope, and Dampier on aborigines span two centuries but illustrate the unchanging contempt for these native people. In the 1790s and early 1800s the aborigines were quickly killed off in Tasmania and pushed inland from the southeastern shores

---

[52] Washburn, "The Moral and Legal Justifications for Dispossessing the Indians," 23.

[53] Dampier is quoted at length in C. M. H. Clark, *A History of Australia, From the Earliest Times to the Age of Macquarie* (Melbourne, 1962), 39–40.

[54] Anthony Trollope, *Australia*, edited by P. D. Edwards and R. B. Joyce (St. Lucia, Queensland, 1967), 113, 475.

[55] *Ibid.*, 475.

[56] Clark, *A History of Australia*, 169.

[57] Quoted from A. T. Yarwood's penetrating essay on Marsden in *Australian Dictionary of Biography* (Melbourne, 1967), II, 209.

of Australia. Although log forts were at first built, the farming and pastoral frontiers soon occupied fertile areas of the interior. Great pastoral estates, the squatters' "stations" as they were called, spread into the hinterlands, widely separated from each other because there was no real military threat from the natives.[58] In 1838 Governor Sir George Gipps divided Port Philip in southern Victoria into four districts. He provided a "protector" for the aborigines after a House of Commons committee reported on the pitiful conditon of these vanishing people, degraded by liquor, disease, and poverty. There is evidence that squatters put arsenic into the natives' flour after the "black savages," as they were called, lighted dry grass with fire sticks, ate sheep or cattle, or occasionally attacked and killed isolated whites.[59] An attempt by the British government to halt the extermination of natives by hanging seven whites who had murdered blacks at a settlement near Myall Creek only made whites more secretive about their punitive raids on the natives.[60] The last Tasmanian woman died in 1888, completing the extinction of her race. As late as the 1890s native police in Queensland were engaging in punitive expeditions against other aborigines.[61] Reservations and missions eventually evolved in

---

[58] Geoffrey Blainey, *The Tyranny of Distance, How Distance Shaped Australia's History* (Melbourne, 1969), 132.

[59] Aboriginals were often referred to as "blacks" or "savages" in newspaper accounts of disturbances and occasional murders of settlers. See, for example, the *Melbourne Argus*, Nov. 20, 1846, p. 2, for an account of troopers capturing three natives, Bobby, Tolmey, and Bullet-eye, all charged with murder. "Poisoning" aborigines "was fairly widespread" according to Bryan W. Harrison, author of a B.A. honors thesis, "The Myall Creek Massacre and Its Significance in the Controversy over the Aborigines During Australia's Early Squatting Period" (New England University, Armidale, 1966), 101–102. On page 102 n., Harrison cites the following publications as evidence of poisoning: *The Colonist*, July 4, 1838; *Sydney Gazette*, Dec. 20, 1838; *Sydney Monitor*, Dec. 24, 1838. The Myall Creek massacre and white use of poisons are briefly covered in C. M. Clark, *A Short History of Australia* (New York, 1963), 87. See also Kathleen Hassel, *The Relations Between the Settlers and Aborigines in South Australia, 1836–60* (Adelaide, 1966), 2 ff.

Whites were reluctant to acknowledge use of poisons against Indians, but, according to Jim Mike, a Ute Indian interviewed on June 20, 1968, the Ute chief, Posey, "was poisoned with flour" in 1923. Doris Duke Tape, 550, Western History Center, University of Utah. Forbes Parkhill, *The Last of the Indian Wars* (New York, 1961), 28–29, 47–48, 70–77, 116, gives the generally accepted interpretation of the last "Ute war" and Posey's death resulting from body wounds.

[60] On the Myall Creek massacre, see note 59, above. On Queensland punitive raids against aborigines, see Price's *White Settlers and Native Peoples*, 138; and Elkin's *The Australian Aborigines*, 323, which states that "pacification" by force continued until the 1930s.

[61] Price, *White Settlers and Native Peoples*, 138; Elkin, *The Australian Aborigines*, 323.

the late nineteenth century but failed to stop the decline of aboriginal population. As one concerned modern Australian describes the story:

When our British forefathers took this land they termed it "waste and unoccupied": in reality they conquered the Aboriginal people by force of arms, disease, starvation and the destruction of Aboriginal social systems. We are heirs to a colonial empire which was built largely on force and a deep abiding belief in the superiority of British people and their institutions.[62]

The author of this encapsulated history of native-white relations has studied the same problem in several areas of the world. He concludes that the Australian policy which first permitted occasional extermination, and then, in the twentieth century, encouraged assimillation is based on "racism," "the conscious or unconscious belief in the basic superiority of individuals of European ancestry, which entitles white peoples to a position of dominance and privilege." He reasons that this attitude not only permitted, but encouraged exploitation of primitive peoples. The policy of assimilation, he argues further, has been based upon ignorance and disdain for the life-style of the aborigines and is concerned only with turning them into "dark-skinned Europeans."[63]

Similar indictments of Europeans in their relations with Indians are in William Christy Macleod's fine volume, *The American Indian Frontier,* and in William Brandon's excellent *The American Heritage Book of Indians.*[64] In America the wars of the forest culminated in Pontiac's uprising in 1763, and, after the Indian conflicts of the American Revolution, there was never again any real threat to white expansion into the interior. The idea of a boundary line separating whites from Indians was rapidly accepted and finally became national policy after Calhoun proposed moving the Indians west of the Mississippi into a permanent reserve.[65] That land was penetrated by the

---

[62] A. Barrie Pittock, *Toward a Multi-Racial Society: The 1969 James Backhouse Lecture* (Pymble, New South Wales, 1969), 5.

[63] *Ibid.,* 12.

[64] The arguments set forth by Macleod and Brandon and other writers are discussed in Jacobs, "British-Colonial Attitudes and Policies Toward the Indian in the American Colonies," 82 ff.

[65] Francis Paul Prucha, *American Indian Policy in the Formative Years: The Indian Trade and Intercourse Acts, 1790–1834* (Cambridge, Mass., 1962), 226–227, 229; Louis De Vorsey, Jr., *The Indian Boundary in the Southern Colonies, 1763–1775* (Chapel Hill, 1966), 27 ff.

massive westward trek of Americans during the 1840s. After fur traders, miners, military leaders, farmers, and railroad builders persuaded
the government that Indians belonged on reservations, the land was
finally subdivided.

As in Australian history, the native was often portrayed as a nomadic
heathen with nasty habits whose beliefs and customs left him virtually
a beast. Such anthropologists as the Australian, A. P. Elkin, and the
American, Nancy O. Lurie, have pointed out that the Europeans who
dispossessed the natives had no appreciation or understanding of native
culture, occupational specialization, social control, or economic concepts. White ideas about native illiteracy, sexual mores, modesty,
Christian beliefs, and white pride in technological superiority (especially the use of guns) buttressed arrogant European assumptions of
superiority.[66] There was no real understanding of the native prefer-
ence for their own culture and way of life over the European system.

For example, the Reverend John Clayton of Virginia in 1687 described the occupation of the male Indians as "exercise," when he
meant hunting. Woman's work, the Reverend Clayton briefly noted,
was gardening, mat weaving, pottery making, and cooking.[67] Clayton's
comments typify those of hundreds of untrained observers who have
given posterity an Indian stereotype: hardworking, industrious women
and lazy, pleasure-loving men. This image also emerges from much
of the Australian and New Guinea literature on native-white contacts. Indeed, it is the impression this writer had when first visiting
Australian aboriginal reserves (in Central Australia, in Queensland,
and in the Darwin area) and primitive villages along the tributaries
of the Sepik River in northern New Guinea. My initial observations
led me to think that men in Swago village in New Guinea spent almost
all their time talking and smoking in their sacred clubhouses, tall,
well-proportioned buildings constructed without nails, called the *haus
tamberam*. Meanwhile the women, it appeared, worked almost as
slaves, caring for children, grinding the pulp of sago palm and strain-
ing it to obtain the white cheeselike starchy food that comprises their
main diet. But I was mistaken, and later found out that the main occupations of the men in the village were varied, physically exhausting,

---

66 Nancy Oestreich Lurie, "Indian Cultural Adjustment to European Civilization," in
Smith, ed., *Seventeenth-Century America*, 38–60.

67 *Ibid.*, 56–60.

and complex, resembling those of the male in an American Indian village. The male in the New Guinea village busied himself with hunting, house and canoe building, the making of artifacts, and participation in a variety of colorful civic and religious ceremonies, many of which concerned the governance and cultural life of the village at large.[68]

So it is today among nomadic aborigines of Central Australia. Similar cultural patterns are found among the Indians of colonial Virginia. According to the anthropologist, Nancy O. Lurie, there were marked similarities between the Indians and the early colonists in male and female division of labor for building houses, hunting, housekeeping, child care, garment making, and cooking.[69] The similarities of both cultures to each other did not lead the white to adopt conciliatory attitudes in the inevitable disputes that arose over occupation of the land. Actually, the stereotype of the Indian in early Virginia history was expanded. Not only was the Indian warrior portrayed as a lazy, pleasure-loving rascal, he was also represented as a treacherous, unclean, pagan savage who ate nasty food and might turn upon one at any time despite his sly professions of friendship.[70] One finds similar stereotypes of New Guinea and Australian aborigines. In American history there are occasional portrayals of Indian nobility and the natural advantages of native life in the forest by such writers as Roger Williams, and such soldiers and Indian superintendents as Robert Rogers and Sir William Johnson.[71] And in Australian history one finds that early European artists drew pictures of manly, athletic, handsome natives, akin to the noble warrior of early Iroquois and Cherokee portraits. However, later pictures of Australian aborigines are almost caricatures, depicting little black people with huge heads, ugly faces, and stick-like legs.[72] Both in Australia and in America the

---

[68] During the summer of 1969, with a native missionary of the Seventh-Day Adventist Church who spoke fluent Pidgin English, I traveled by outboard motorboat some sixty miles beyond the Sepik River town of Ambunti to Swago village, an interior jungle settlement located on a small tributary of the Sepik. Here, with two other visiting whites, I lived for several days in one of the most primitive, isolated native villages in Papua-New Guinea.

[69] Lurie, "Indian Cultural Adjustment to European Civilization," 57.

[70] *Ibid.*, 38–39.

[71] Jacobs, "British-Colonial Attitudes," 86–90.

[72] John D. Cross of the Mitchell Library staff in Sydney has called my attention to eighteenth-century drawings of aborigines as exemplified by artists who were with Captain Cook. Here we have heroic, masculine figures. Later portrayals of the aborigines,

contemptuous stereotype seems to have submerged the favorable portrait in order to help rationalize unjust policies.

Misconceptions about both American Indians and Australian aborigines were based upon ignorance of native culture and its development after it confronted white society. There was little in the European's technology that the Indians in Virginia could not evaluate in terms of their own experience. They had made copper ornaments. As soon as they became accustomed to the noisy blast of firing, they familiarized themselves with guns as well as other metal tools. Similarly, fabrics were a part of native technology, and Indians had already made their own nets, weirs, and garden tools. English ships, to Indians, were much like big canoes. Indian religion was polytheistic, based upon a pantheon, and thus a Christian deity could be added, just as the Indians could adopt the use of guns, needles, and scissors. What whites had difficulty in comprehending was that many of the seventeenth and eighteenth-century Indians viewed themselves as equal to the Europeans. Although they would borrow a deity or a technological innovation, they were for the most part unimpressed with the trappings of European civilization.[73] Even those colonial sachems and chiefs who had been to England failed to urge the white man's ways on their fellow tribesmen.[74]

Indians of the colonial period did not consider assimilation a solution to the problem of dealing with the whites. This path would have meant servitude, perhaps slavery, educational programs, adoption of their children, and possibly intermarriage, all proposed by Europeans at one time or another during the colonial era. The Indian solution was to attempt to remove the source of anxiety by direct attack on the whites. Pontiac's aim, in the great Indian war of 1763, was to drive the British frontier back into the sea.[75] The Indians who fought the English during the 1760s were fighting for self-determination. For generations they had governed themselves in their towns and villages. Their fortifications and buildings were impressive, even to the colonists.

---

especially in the 1840s, depict them almost as monkeys with thin legs and potbellies. Examples of both kinds of drawings are in Moorehead, *The Fatal Impact*, 144–145. Perhaps the best overall study on noble savage imagery in the South Pacific is Bernard Smith, *European Vision of the South Pacific, 1768–1850* (New York, 1960).

73 Lurie, "Indian Cultural Adjustment to European Civilization," 38–39.

74 *Ibid.* Little Carpenter, Cherokee chief who visited England, remembered only "kind Promises" that were made to him. William L. McDowell, Jr., ed., *Documents relating to Indian Affairs, 1754–1765: Colonial Records of South Carolina* (Columbia, S.C., 1970), 138.

75 Jacobs, "Was the Pontiac Uprising A Conspiracy?," 26–37.

Gardens, orchards, and grain fields attested to their agricultural skill. Indians had no desire to abandon their own culture. The Cherokee who made a last stand against the English in 1760 were such expert farmers that William Wirt, their legal defender in the later controversy over their removal to the far West in 1830, found whites fearful that Indian skills would prevent Georgia's occupation of Cherokee land. The Georgians insisted upon regarding the Cherokee as hunters and argued that these Indians "had no right to alter their condition to become husbandmen."[76] This remarkable argument denies, of course, the right of the Cherokee to become farmers within the area of Georgian territory. Georgia's argument was carried forward until "it was made clear that, though the Georgian soil was destined to be tilled, it was destined to be tilled by the white man and not the Indian."[77] Thus, white racist rationale was employed to justify taking lands occupied by the Cherokee, one of the great Indian people who had tilled the land for centuries. Dispossession of nomadic plains Indians or seizure of lands occupied by the more primitive California Indians required no such Byzantine reasoning. Whites could call upon John Locke and the "Creator" to justify their land grabs.

At least the early record of Canada in dealing with the Indians is notably better than that of the United States. The fur trading tradition of the Hudson's Bay Company and Montreal required that understanding and friendship be maintained with the Indians if the resources of the land were to be successfully exploited. Thus in Canadian relations with the Indians, private or exclusive occupation of the land was not necessary or even desirable in most areas.[78] In both the

---

76 Quoted in Weinberg, *Manifest Destiny*, 86–87.

77 *Ibid.* The relatively unknown story of the dispossession of the Indians of the Far West during the Mexican War era is told in Robert Anthony Trennert, "The Far Western Indian Frontier and the Beginnings of the Reservation System, 1846–1851" (Ph.D. dissertation, University of California, Santa Barbara, 1969). Trennert discusses "the policy of extermination long advocated by many Texans" (p. 152) and the bitterly fought Texas Indian wars of 1846–1851 (pp. 113–154, 320–364).

78 George Simpson, Hudson's Bay Company executive, repeatedly emphasizes in his journals the importance of the Indian in the company's fur trade enterprises. He even goes so far as to consider "the effect the conversion of Indians might have on the trade," concluding that it would not be "injurious," and indeed might be "highly beneficial" if it caused the Indians to be "more industrious, more seriously . . . [concerned with] the Chase." Frederick Merk, ed., *Fur Trade and Empire, George Simpson's Journal . . . , 1824–1825* (Cambridge, Mass., 1968), 108–109. On the company's price wars which resulted from American trading ships contacting Indians, see John S. Galbraith, *The Hudson's Bay Company As An Imperial Factor, 1821–69* (Berkeley, 1957), 138–140. A

United States and Australia, however, the persistent clamor of the pioneers for land was the basic factor in the desire of frontier settlers to rid themselves of aboriginal people.[79]

In New Guinea, as we have seen, the indigenous people were never conquered and dispossessed of their lands. They were saved from the worst evils of white racism and possible decimation. Geography, climate, and the physical and cultural vitality of these and other native people all played a part in determining the fate of individual tribes in their confrontation with whites. Europeans, sometimes brutalized by their own cruelty toward aborigines when the opportunity for gain was present, have yet to seek accommodation. This may be found in understanding the land ethic of the native people which allowed them to depend upon an economy closely governed by the ecology of the surrounding wilderness.

Yet nations today that are led by a powerful white citizenry are still often unsympathetic to the aspirations of native peoples. For instance, the popularity of Frederick Jackson Turner's frontier theory in North America and in Australia is evidence of the historians' concern for the development of white civilization and the exploitation of the land. Native peoples play only a minor role in this widely accepted interpretation. Turner, in his influential essay of 1893, dismissed the Indian as "a consolidating agent" who helped to encourage intercolonial cooperation for border defense.[80] Turner also treated Indians in his lectures as if they were some kind of geographical obstacle to the westward movement of whites.[81] Australian and British writers who have applied the Turner theory to Australian history sometimes equate

---

House of Commons report of 1857 strongly supported the company's desire to maintain a monopoly for the "protection of the natives against the evils of openly competitive bidding and for conservation of fur-bearing animals." Quoted in Douglas MacKay, *The Honourable Company, A History of the Hudson's Bay Company* (New York, 1936), 274. However, as Simpson's journal demonstrates, the company's concern with profits was such that it would not follow a policy of conservation of fur-bearing animals, even when the supply was being "unremittingly hunted" to exhaustion in certain areas. See Merk, ed., *Fur Trade and Empire*, 151–152.

79 H. C. Allen, *Bush and Backwoods: A Comparison of the Frontier in Australia and the United States* (Sydney, 1959), 24–25; John Wesley Powell, "From Warpath to Reservation," in Wilcomb E. Washburn, ed., *The Indian and the White Man* (New York, 1964), 377–391; R. M. W. Reece, "The Aborigines and Colonial Society in New South Wales Before 1850, With Special Reference to the Period of the Gipps Administration, 1838–1846" (M. A. thesis, University of Queensland, 1969), 10–143.

80 Frederick Jackson Turner, *The Frontier in American History* (New York, 1921), 15.

81 Jacobs, "British Colonial Attitudes," 106.

the Blue Mountains with the Blue Ridge range and the bushranger with the mountain man, but they are hard pressed to explain the Australian character as an outgrowth of occasional conflicts with the aborigines, because the fighting was so completely one-sided.[82] A leading Australian historian tells us, without tongue in cheek, that the timid, peaceful Aborigines may have helped to bring a friendly, law-abiding society to Australia where whites usually settle their quarrels without violence.[83] Be that as it may, Indians and aborigines have surely influenced the course of history in America and Australia more than is often recognized, if only by giving a special tincture to the society of the whites who occupied their lands. There are no writers at the University of Papua-New Guinea who see Turner's frontier theory as applicable to that country, for it largely belongs to the indigenous people. The frontier theory, an interpretation of the development of white characteristics in a new land, cannot be applied to a country where the natives still control the mass of their own land and outnumber the Europeans.

The frontier theory, then, represents not only an interpretation of history but also an attitude that historians have taken toward the land, native people, and the expansion of white civilization. As has been mentioned, white attitude toward native people is often a powerful factor in determining governmental policies. In Papua-New Guinea today, the Australian government, under the spotlight of the United Nations and as trustee for an underdeveloped country, has made great strides in giving the native people what might be called a "fair deal" in social services, land policies, and in self-government. This accords with the attitudes of many enlightened Australians whose influence has been so powerful that Australian public opinion now supports fair treatment for the aborigines at home.[84]

---

82 Australian writers have perhaps been less successful in making a hero out of the "bushman" or "bushranger." See Russell Ward, *Australia* (London, 1965), 9, 58–59, 94–96. Ward develops the bushranger myth more fully in his readable volume, *The Australian Legend* (Melbourne, 1961). Romantic myths have also grown up around the picturesque Brazilian bandeirrantes, jungle pathfinders whose movements were governed by Indian slave hunting and prospecting cycles. Richard M. Morse, ed., *The Bandeirrantes: The Historical Role of the Brazilian Pathfinders* (New York, 1965), 5, 23, 181–190.

83 Ward, *Australia*, 27.

84 All aborigines are now citizens, and in theory possess the voting franchise and are eligible for a whole range of social service benefits. Dept. of Territories, *The Australian Aborigines*, (Sydney, 1967), 66–110. Yet I observed that aboriginal people are still deprived of their civil rights as in the case of the reserve at Palm Island off the

The fact that the New Guineans still retain most of their land and cultural heritage is probably due to chance, a fortunate combination of circumstances that enabled them to withstand the frontier of white advance. A different set of circumstances allowed European greed to prevail over tolerance on the frontiers of Australia and North America. If we condemn the white man in his relations with the Indians and the Australian aborigines, we must be aware that the same kind of abominations can occur again if the stakes are high enough. A case in point is the future policy of the United States in recognizing oil, mineral, and land claims of Alaskan Indians and Eskimos. Americans have not created a society in which greed is not a controlling motivation. If different races are to live together in harmony in a pluralistic society, then they must free themselves from the urge to look down upon what may seem to be an inferior way of life.

We must also try to understand nativist movements that are often-times supported by people whose older values have been lost and whose new ambitions are difficult to achieve. In Australia, in New Guinea, and among the American Indians there are such activist native movements. We should be reluctant to portray these activities as Communist inspired for there is a fundamental difference between the ancient native communalism and modern Marxist Communism. We must realize that modern nativist activism has its basis in a real disagreement with a white man's culture that has taken so much and given so little.[85]

It is only recently that we are beginning to understand the dilemma of fourth world oppressed minorities, some of them tribal people living within the borders of "third world" developing nations as well as industrially advanced nations such as the United States and Australia.[86] For tribal peoples, the advance of European nation states into

---

coast of Queensland at Townsville. Here the administration seems to be entirely under the Queensland police and an executive officer who was formerly a plantation manager. There is a substantial body of literature on present aboriginal problems. See, for example, *We the Australians: What is to Follow the Referendum? Proceedings of the Inter-Racial Seminar held at Townsville, December, 1967* (Townsville, 1968); Frank Stevens, *Equal Wages for Aborigines, The Background to Industrial Discrimination in the Northern Territory of Australia* (Sydney, 1968); T. G. H. Strehlow, *Assimilation Problems: The Aboriginal Viewpoint* (Adelaide, 1964); Frank Hardy, *The Unlucky Australians* (Sydney, 1968), 175–209.

85 Douglas Oliver in his perceptive, searching study of natives of the Pacific also makes this point. See *The Pacific Islands*, 425–426.

86 A Minorities Rights Group (MRG) was formed in London in 1970, with the plan of assisting "the position of persecuted or disadvantaged ethnic, religious or cultural minori-

virgin lands during the age of exploration was the beginning of a long era of hardship, dispossession, and depopulation.[87]

---

ties . . . in any country." The MRG Director, Ben Whitaker, has recently edited *The Fourth World: Victims of Group Oppression: Eight Reports from the Field Work of the Minority Rights Group* (New York, 1973) concentrating on the dilemma of Fourth World peoples in Sudan, Rhodesia, Brazil, the Soviet Union, and other nations. Although native American Indian peoples are not included in this volume, it is obvious that they face many of the same pressing difficulties of minorities in other areas of the globe.

[87] For a discussion of controversies surrounding the new population estimated of native American Indians in 1492 and the "demographic disaster" that followed, see W. R. Jacobs, "The Tip of the Iceberg: Pre-Columbian Indian Demography and Some Implications for Revisionism," *William and Mary Quarterly*, XXXI (1974), 123–132. In this same issue is a brilliant, interdisciplinary study on a related theme, Calvin Martin's essay, "The European Impact on the Culture of a Northeastern Indian Tribe: An Ecological Interpretation," *ibid.*, 3–26.

The World's Oldest On-Going Protest Demonstration: North American Indian Drinking Patterns

NANCY OESTREICH LURIE

The author, a member of the anthropology department in the University of Wisconsin, Milwaukee, offers in this article valuable insights to historians.

W HEN I READ Craig MacAndrew and Robert Edgerton's *Drunken Comportment,* I felt a bit as Alfred Russell Wallace must have felt upon learning about the work of Charles Darwin. I had presented an initial version of this paper at an anthropological meeting shortly before receiving a copy of *Drunken Comportment.* The book validates beyond question some of my early speculations and documents in detail my historical generalizations. However, it concentrates on one item of "conventional wisdom" while my paper is directed at another.

The apparently self-evident common sense which MacAndrew and Edgerton systematically demolish is the widely held notion of the public and temperance societies—and even many medically and psychiatrically oriented researchers—that alcohol disinhibits and causes

I want to thank John Boatman, a sociology graduate student at the University of Wisconsin–Milwaukee, 1968–1969, who brought to my attention a number of the sources cited and inspired me to work up the ideas that resulted in this publication. I would also like to thank other Indian friends who commented on the first draft of this paper and helped me to clarify some of the concepts. Of course, any shortcomings and misinterpretations are my responsibility.

what they term personality "changes-for-the-worse." In case after well documented case from all over the world, MacAndrew and Edgerton demonstrate conclusively that the unquestioned physiological effect (i.e., sensorimotor dysfunction) which accompanies the ingestion of alcohol is given different cultural interpretations by different peoples. These interpretations are manifested in different kinds of locally patterned, learned forms of drunkenness ranging from changes-for-the-worse to changes-for-the-better.[1] The authors also point out that the widespread occurrence of drunken disinhibition and changes-for-the-worse are not evidence of any inherent quality of alcohol, as conventional wisdom assumes; alcohol has merely been diffused to many peoples across the world by the adventurers of western society who also introduced their own cultural patterns of drunken behavior.

Accepting MacAndrew and Edgerton's findings, I would like to challenge the conventional wisdom concerning American Indian drinking that starts out with the assumption that real American Indian identity is only preserved in museums and that Indians drink because of an identity crisis. According to such thinking, Indian culture has just about phased out, if it is not entirely gone, and excessive drinking by the minority group that still persists as Indian must be due to low self-esteem, feelings of rejection, and the effects of prejudice and material deprivation vis à vis white, middle-class culture and society. It is only common sense, according to this argument, that Indians get drunk to escape into a glorified, romanticized past and try to regain a sense of identity as Indians, at least temporarily, because they encounter so many difficulties in assimilating into and being accepted by the dominant group and its culture. This layman's view is even shared by scholars as a recent publication of the Canadian Alcohol and Drug Addiction Research Foundation demonstrates: "drinking . . . activities are explicable as responses to acculturation anxieties and as substitutes for previously institutionalized interaction."[2] Similar arguments are advanced by J. H. Hamer and Bernard J. James.

. . . drinking . . . permits persons temporarily to assume desirable status positions when there has been interference with, and inadequate substitutes for, the traditional social structure. . . .[3]

---

[1] Craig MacAndrew and Robert B. Edgerton, *Drunken Comportment, A Social Explanation* (Chicago, 1969), 13–36.

[2] *Culture and Alcohol Use: A Bibliography of Anthropological Studies* (Ottawa, 1966), 1.

[3] J. H. Hamer, "Acculturation Stress and the Functions of Alcohol Among the Forest County Potawatomi," *Quarterly Journal of Studies on Alcohol*, XXVI (1965), 285.

. . . Ojibwa culture . . . has become deculturated and . . . its minimal appropriation of new cultural traits has produced a "poor White" type of subculture. . . . The anxiety that casts it[s] shadow across the entire gamut of Ojibwa behavior is a product of both the physical deprivations that attend reservation experience . . . as well as the conflicts and uncertainties that characterize status inferiority. . . . Alcohol acts to reduce the sense of isolation and to permit the ventilation of anxieties. . . .[4]

Marshall Clinard draws the same general conclusion when he insists that "the primary problem from which 'problem drinking' has its genesis is the strain which structural barriers or prohibitions put upon the realization of success goals." [5] Perhaps he is right, but it is pertinent to ask in the case of Indian drinking whether we know which success goals are being thwarted.

As Indian people struggle for a workable cultural and social pluralism, adapting contemporary American economic necessities and some of the amenities to their own systems of values, their strivings seem to be frequently misunderstood. Although at the present time Indian spokesmen are gaining a wider hearing, their insistence that they want to be *Indians* still tends either to be dismissed by "practical" whites as being as unrealistic as trying to bring back the buffalo or encouraged by "sympathetic" whites as envisioning an actual return to the kind of Indian life depicted in museums. When Indian people begin to bring off what they evidently have in mind, improvement of their material welfare on their own terms, their success is interpreted as fulfilling the highly individualistic aspirations of middle-class white society and as a stepping stone to total absorption into it.

All of the authorities cited and many others besides advert to the stereotype, designated a negative stereotype, of the "drunken Indian." I find that their observational data support my conclusions better than their own. There are two points that are glossed over. First, there is a positive stereotype of the noble Red Man that is supposedly the identity which Indians seek in drunken delusions but which is actually exploited by cold-sober Indians who lecture and engage in theatrical performances. Rather than denying Indians this identity and thereby compelling them to seek it in alcohol, the larger society accepts and promotes it as evidenced by Boy Scouts and similar groups who even

---

4 Bernard J. James, "Social-Psychological Dimensions of Ojibwa Acculturation," *American Anthropologist*, LXII (1961), 728, 735, 741.

5 Marshall B. Clinard, ed., *Anomie and Deviant Behavior: A Discussion and Critique* (New York, 1964), 202.

play this kind of stereotypic Indian. Secondly, while we have the stereotype of the "drunken Indian," we do not have the "drunken Negro" or the "drunken poor white," the latter group otherwise considered analogous to Indians by Bernard J. James.[6] These other minorities may not drink at all, or they may drink as much as Indians and get just as drunk, but neither their own spokesmen nor concerned outsiders see such drinking as a special problem of the minorities.

In trying to get ahead in terms of white success goals, black people particularly have suffered far more of the indignities, prejudice, rejection, and disappointments which are used to explain why Indian people drink. Black people are also stereotyped negatively but in ways distinct from the Indian stereotype—childlike, irresponsible about property, and dangerous if not "kept in their place." In the nascent and early stages of the black civil rights movement, as eventually given explicit expression by Martin Luther King, black people tried to justify their demands for fair and equal treatment by promoting an ideal image of themselves as ambitious, hard working, and in their forebearance outdoing the white man at his own game of Christian ethics. The dominant society would not accept this stereotype. Once black non-violence was organized, however, it communicated itself as violence and was met with violence. This was returned in kind by black people who then began getting results. It is now common knowledge that even middle-class black people believe the riots and civil disturbances did more good than harm, despite the fact that these people might deplore the need for violence and not engage in it personally. Black violence, like Indian drinking, communicates in mutually understood terms in the respective inter-group confrontations. The negative stereotype of the black, like the "drunken Indian," becomes a virtue or useful weapon to the in-group so stereotyped, at least up to the point of demanding attention and getting action. "Internalization" of the negative stereotype—that is, accepting it and even acting it out—does not, as James would have it, lead the Indian person "to conclude that he is, in fact, an 'inferior' person." [7] Quite the contrary. Indian people appear to have long understood what blacks have recently discovered: the value of the negative stereotype as a form of communication and protest demonstration to register opposition and

6 James, "Social-Psychological Dimensions of Ojibwa Acculturation," 733.
7 Ibid., 732.

hold the line against what they do not want until they can get what they do want.

My hypothesis, then, begins with the assumption that Indian people want to persist and succeed on their own terms as Indians, while at the same time borrowing freely from the material aspects of white culture. It does not matter to the hypothesis whether this is a good thing or whether in the opinion of the non-Indian they succeed. The fact is that they have maintained this sentiment and have endured for well over a century in the face of public expectation that they would vanish, and despite official policies and programs that have been directed explicitly toward phasing them out. My hypothesis is that Indian drinking is an established means of asserting and validating Indianness and will be either a managed and culturally patterned recreational activity or else not engaged in at all in direct proportion to the availability of other effective means of validating Indianness.[8] Three other means of validating contemporary Indianness will be dealt with in some detail later on as a preliminary test of the hypothesis.

In testing the hypothesis, my research design requires that we treat Indian drinking as a cultural artifact, applying Ralph Linton's four-part analysis of artifacts—form, function, meaning, and use.[9] The "form" of Indian drinking (as opposed to other kinds of drinking Indians may also indulge in) is getting purposefully drunk to confirm the stereotype of the drunken Indian. Its function, that is, its relationship to other aspects of the culture or the culture as a whole, is maintenance of the Indian-white boundary by conveying a message: "like it or not,

---

8 I want to stress what I mean by validating since an earlier version of this paper was apparently misunderstood. Vine Deloria, Jr., in his *We Talk, You Listen* (New York, 1970), 10, writes: " . . . last summer a noted female anthropologist presented a scholarly paper to the effect that Indians drink to gain an identity." Deloria goes on to demonstrate the absurdity of such an idea, and I fully agree that it is absurd because I never made such an assertion. In fact, I wrote my paper to combat the idea he attributes to me. Let me explain my position by an analogy. I have no doubt whatsoever about my identity. I am completely secure on this score. But I, like anyone else, often have to validate my identity to do what I want to do; for example, I must produce a driver's license to cash a check. Indian people when among other Indians, as Deloria notes, often cite tribal identity to validate their claims as Indians among strange Indians. There are other times when people may accept that I am who I say I am but may make assumptions that I consider unwarranted and undesirable in defining what kind of a person I am. As a woman and an academic among other things, I engage in all kinds of symbolic behavior in dress and manner that I usually do not even think about but rely on as devices my culture provides to communicate things about myself which will be clearly understood.

9 Ralph Linton, *The Study of Man* (New York, 1936), 402–404.

I am an Indian." Its meaning, the affective part, is to feel good or at least better. This is often verbalized, as many anthropologists and others can attest from personal observation, but I believe the wording is frequently misconstrued. When Indian people say they drink "to feel like an Indian" or words to that effect, I am not convinced of the conventional interpretation that they are seeking identity in drunken delusions of living in the golden past or expressing sheer bottle courage against white presumptions of superiority. Indian drinking plays upon the notion, widely shared by Indians and non-Indians, that Indians "can't hold their liquor like white men." Untenable physiologically, this belief, nevertheless, has a good deal of functional utility in communicating in mutually understood terms.[10] Finally, the "use" of Indian drinking, the way an artifact is manipulated, employed or applied, is to get drunk according to prescribed form with greater or lesser frequency or intensity as it is called for situationally among one's own people, other tribes, or white society. Drinking to get drunk may make a person feel good in terms of a very old shared recreational activity of the Indian community. This may not be the non-Indians' idea of good, clean fun but on close analysis it can be seen to be carefully managed without real personal or social harm.[11] Drunkenness may also be an effort to relieve frustration when other means of asserting Indianness are not readily available. Not so well managed in these cases in regard to personal and social side effects, such drinking is still within its own cultural framework of patterned and calculated bad behavior and understood as such by other Indians and even whites in terms of the stereotype of the drunken Indian.

Before discussing alternatives to drunkenness as means of validating Indianness, I would like to comment on a number of features of Indian drinking which are pertinent to the hypothesis and gave rise to it. Despite acceptance of the stereotype even by Indian people that they cannot hold their liquor like whites, it does not take very extensive field work to observe that the irresponsible drunk on one occasion may on another occasion ingest just as much or more alcohol and maintain an

---

10 MacAndrew and Edgerton, *Drunken Comportment,* chaps. 6 and 7. In these chapters, both entitled "Indians Can't Hold Their Liquor," the authors analyze the factual untenableness but functional utility of this popular belief.

11 Wesley Hurt, "Social Drinking Patterns Among The Yankton Sioux," *Human Organizations,* XXIV (1965), 222–230. This is one of the few ethnographic studies which views drinking among Indians as an established cultural complex rather than a "problem."

appearance of sobriety. Indian people, like anyone else, have differential capacities for alcohol. What is important in any case are the specific social conditions relevant to differences in behavior. My own observations suggest that Indian people are more likely to get drunk when they feel thwarted in achieving Indian rather than white goals or when their success as Indians or simply individuals apart from Indian-white comparisons is interpreted as success in achieving status as whites.

Indian suggestibility to drunkenness has been widely observed as has the Indian community's ambivalence toward drunkenness which seems to be related to the suggestibility. Drinking and drunkenness are deplored on the one hand, while the drunk is treated tolerantly on the other. People may withdraw from the obstreperous drunk to lessen his destructive impact on others but do not hold him seriously responsible for criminal and asocial acts as if he were sober. J. O. Whittaker's observations on the Standing Rock Sioux apply quite generally: "social sanctions against the heavy drinker or alcoholic are virtually nonexistent."[12] Possibly some community tolerance is due to the fact that many Indian people have similar problems and can empathize with the drunk's behavior vicariously while still being forced to recognize that the drunk is a community nuisance. The question remains, what is it the drunk is trying to accomplish that other Indian people understand and thus tolerate? I believe there is a "good" message in drunkenness no matter how "bad" the individual drunk may be. The community regrets the need for drunkenness just as the middle-class black deplores the need for violence to achieve given ends. There is also the realization that, in actualizing the stereotype or becoming habituated to its use and overlooking other alternatives to achieve given ends, undesirable side effects may offset the original idea intended by the demonstration. As Edward Dozier notes, many Indian communities have sought to reduce the problem by making liquor harder to get:

... the prohibition of liquor by tribal councils on most Indian reservations after repeal of the federal restrictive law is indicative of the Indians' own concern about abuses in drinking. . . .[13]

---

12 J. O. Whittaker, "Alcohol and the Standing Rock Sioux Tribe, II: Psychodynamics and Cultural Factors in Drinking," *Quarterly Journal of Studies on Alcohol*, XXIV (1963), 90.

13 Edward P. Dozier, "Problem Drinking Among American Indians: The Role of Sociocultural Deprivation," *Quarterly Journal of Studies on Alcohol*, XXVII (1966), 73.

Similarly, North American revitalization movements, such as the religion of Handsome Lake among the Iroquois and the pan-Indian Native American Church (peyote), interdict liquor while endeavoring to assert Indianness by means of such alternatives as the revival of customs and use of objects that are unmistakably derived from Indian tradition. Such religions assume that Indians are by nature different and cannot hold their liquor like whites.[14] Where no such movement of this kind provides strong group assertions of Indians' rights to be Indians, it is difficult for the community to bring strong pressures to bear to discourage drinking, the more so because of widespread Indian reluctance to question anyone else's personal decisions. It is deemed better if temptation is simply removed as much as possible.

But even if the supply of liquor is reduced, it is not difficult for people to get drunk if they are determined to do so. The usefulness of feigned drunkenness, whether consciously or subconsciously engaged in, doubtlessly helps to explain the familiar Indian suggestibility to drunkenness. Whittaker's statements on the Standing Rock Sioux are again applicable to many Indian communities. Aggressive behavior is "virtually unknown in sober individuals" while "drunkenness, on the other hand, is frequently associated with violence."[15] Statistics on Indian criminality demonstrate that Indians have a high arrest rate, that crime is almost always alcohol related, and that the crimes are largely unplanned and often terribly conspicuous offenses.[16] While I have no argument with universalistic frustration-aggression theory, I suggest that if you are an Indian and need to work off frustrations, whatever their cause, you are doubly frustrated. Your stereotype of whites is that *they* are aggressive. As J. H. Hamer has observed, and I believe correctly, drinking gives the Indian person "an escape from

---

Dozier implies ideas made explicit here; deprivation of the opportunity to be an Indian is fundamental to so-called problem drinking rather than deprivation of white status, which is the approach of Bernard J. James cited above. It is perhaps significant that Dozier is himself an Indian.

14 This generalization is based on personal familiarity with members of the religions. As far as published work is concerned, the best discussion of Handsome Lake can be found in Anthony F. C. Wallace's *The Death and Rebirth of The Seneca* (New York, 1970), especially Part III. On the peyote religion, the best book is J. Sydney Slotkin's *The Peyote Religion* (Glencoe, 1956). Significantly, Handsome Lake and John Rave, the Winnebago who provided much of the inspiration for the institutionalization of peyote in the Native American Church, were both notorious drunkards before conversion.

15 Whittaker, "Alcohol and the Standing Rock Sioux," 85.

16 Omer Stewart, "Questions Regarding American Indian Criminality," *Human Organization*, XXIII (1964), 61–66.

anxiety about the expression of overt aggression."[17] Thus, before giving vent to aggressive inclinations, you get drunk or convince yourself and others you are drunk, in order that no one mistakes you for acting like a white man. James, with whom I took issue at the outset, provides what I consider a telling incident in this connection although I think he draws entirely erroneous conclusions from it.

... a band of carousing [Ojibwa] villagers broke into a church and its tabernacle in search of wine. The aisles of the building were left littered with beer cans. While such sacrilegious outbursts shock the community, there is no clear evidence that they are triggered by hostile feelings toward the mission. They seem to be the result simply of the lust for drink.[18]

The beer cans strike me as rather elaborate evidence to show that the carousers were already drunk when they broke into the church.

James and others who subscribe to the idea that Indians drink because they have a low sense of self-esteem and are seeking identity rely on phrases like those I have also collected in the course of field research: "I can't get ahead because I'm an Indian" or "I'm as good as any white man." I feel such expressions of sentiment are used selectively and misconstrued. To me, they seem of a piece with other phrases having nothing to do with anxieties over status deprivation in assimilating into white society. In the course of collecting more data on Indian drinking than I ever sought, it has struck me that the Winnebago tribesman is as likely to say, "I'm as good as any Potawatomi" as "I'm as good as any white man." Friend Potawatomi answers in kind, sometimes with a punch in the nose to make his point that he is as good as any Winnebago. Despite the young Indian nationalists' insistence that Indians should identify first as Indians and then by tribe, tribal affiliation remains the primary means of establishing identity. There is also the oft heard challenge, "I'm a bigger Indian than you are," or, put sarcastically, "You big Indian, you!" The challenge is more philosophical than physical since such phrases are simply "Englished-out" of native languages and often not understood by the non-Indian observer who, if he thinks about it at all, puts his own interpretation on what he hears. What is really meant, in effect, is "I'm more genuinely Indian than you are."

---

17 Hamer, "Acculturation Stress and the Functions of Alcohol Among the Forest County Potawatomi," 285.

18 James, "Social-Psychological Dimensions of Ojibwa Acculturation," 731.

This is not to deny the existence of classic self-hate and identity crises among Indian people as among other minority groups. However, in my own experience these are most frequently found among families or individuals who are estranged from the life of their Indian communities and would like to treat their obvious Indian ancestry as their white neighbors might advert to Norway or Ireland or some other "old country" beyond which they feel they have progressed. They acknowledge their origins, even with pride and some cultural tokens, but this has little to do with the everyday business of contemporary American life or even the contemporary cultures whence their ancestors came. If such Indian people can only manage to be genteely poor, then there is no question that they suffer low self-esteem and a sense of deprivation. They may even get drunk for these familiar reasons, thus supporting conventional wisdom and nullifying my hypothesis in such cases. However, I find they are often the very people least likely to get drunk or drink at all. Are they perhaps afraid of being mistaken for *Indians?*

Likewise, feelings of frustration and inadequacy in white society are commonly expressed by perfectly sober Indian students who are in a state of anxious ambivalence created largely by the school situation where white authority figures and peers badger them directly and indirectly to stop being Indians. They are made to feel by their own people that staying in school and succeeding as well as white students is a kind of betrayal. This is difficult to understand for well intentioned white people, including scholars, who have never been praised, overtly or subtly, for their apparent denial, lack, or denigration of their "whiteness." Finally, I would like to turn to historical considerations and show the evolution of Indian drinking from an institutionalized "time-out" period from ordinary canons of etiquette (a function it still serves on occasion) to its gradually expanding function of communication and protest in order to maintain the Indian-white boundary.

Liquor, of course, was a novelty to all North American Indian tribes except for a very few southwestern groups.[19] It also proved to be an exceedingly attractive novelty. Too often frontier histories suggest

---

19 Among these few tribes were the Papago. MacAndrew and Edgerton, in *Drunken Comportment*, 37–42, document how native cactus wine was used in Papago religious ceremonies to promote a state of harmony with nature and one's fellow man which the Papago deemed generally desirable but impossible to achieve in the course of secular life. In other words, drunken behavior was characterized by changes-for-the-better. In-

that the introduction of liquor to the Indians led only to wild, drunken orgies. This view is contradicted by the numerous primary sources cited by MacAndrew and Edgerton on the first encounters of many Indians with alcohol.[20] They show that the inevitable sensorimotor dysfunctions were given widely varying interpretations, ranging from apparent delight in "instant vision" to repugnance. As liquor was "pushed" by traders and became generally available, some, perhaps many, Indians never developed a taste for it, but, for those who did, cultural patterns of drunkenness became apparent which included expansive conviviality, the letting down of customary decorum, and, in some cases, serious dignified drinking into a comatose state. In time the drunken behavior of traders and other adventurers was emulated

---

troduced to the trader's whiskey and the white man's disinhibited changes-for-the-worse, the Papago got drunk in emulation of their white mentors. Meanwhile, their religious use of cactus wine with its expected results continued. Different kinds of drunken behavior were manifested by the same people in different socio-cultural situations.

20 *Ibid.*, 100–135. There seems to have been a considerable time *after* the first encounter with alcohol before an Indian group gave evidence of really debauched drinking, and even then all the accounts of drinking bouts are not of this nature. We need more intensive historical study of recorded Indian drinking sessions in chronological sequence, following the moving frontier from tribe to tribe and from such contact to the present, including a search for data on inter-tribal diffusion of drinking customs. MacAndrews and Edgerton make clear that white historians tend to accept any mention of an Indian drinking bout as bearing out the stereotype of the aggressive, destructive, violent drunken Indian, whereas, in actual fact, the chroniclers of these occasions presented a range of descriptions which should be studied more carefully. As the Indians lost their lands and power, there may have been a discernible shift from using drunkenness as a simple, relaxed "time-out" period to using it as an occasion to commit serious asocial and criminal acts. As it became harder to express aggression effectively against whites and frustration mounted, aggression may well be shown to have turned increasingly inward. This possibility is certainly in keeping with fairly well established frustration-aggression theory. In this context, it should be noted that Clyde Kluckhohn explains native Indian belief in witchcraft in this fashion in his "Navaho Witchcraft," *Papers of the Peabody Museum of Archeology and Ethnology*, XXII (1944). Fear, suspicion, accusations, and even hanging of alleged witches increased during the second half of the nineteenth century as the Navahos came increasingly under white domination. Witchcraft is a widespread, remarkably uniform cultural complex in much of North America, suggesting a very old cultural stratum. I have been struck by the apparent similarity between the growth of witchcraft among the Navajo, as described by Kluckhohn, and its increase among Great Lakes tribes, who use it to explain such problems as sickness and the inability to overcome poverty. There, too, it seems to be an outlet for aggression in the face of frustration. Drunkenness has an advantage over witchcraft in that drunken aggression to some extent can be directed against white society as well as inward. Since most whites believe that "Indians can't hold their liquor," there is a mutually understandable way to communicate protest and hostility. Whites do not understand Indian witchcraft and, if they learn about it at all, they tend to draw false analogies to what they consider "old fashioned" European superstition about old women riding with their black cats on broomsticks.

and improved upon by Indian people, but—and this is the point I wish to emphasize—they seem to have done so for cultural reasons of their own. These reasons relate to a number of entrenched, ubiquitous Indian values and ideals which transcend tribal considerations.

Recorded in the earliest documents, the Indian values are still noted in contemporary field studies as explicit ideals which are manifested in Indian behavior.[21] Primary among these attributes are the beliefs that one is expected to take full responsibility for his own actions,[22] to exhibit concern for personal dignity, to take pride in resourcefulness and to adapt what is at hand in order to survive, to demonstrate open-handed generosity and gracious acceptance of proffered gifts (essentially a strong sense of reciprocity),[23] and to show "respect" for other people. Some observers interpret the last as "permissiveness," a view which I consider too simplistic; it is simply too difficult for most whites to keep their noses out of other people's business, especially if they think they are saving people from their own shortcomings. These core values may have become demanding beyond their functional utility by the time of white contact, and thus drunkenness, in the form of disinhibited changes-for-the-worse, may have been seized upon in the way that Christianity was readily accepted and adopted by the taboo ridden Hawaiian aristocracy. The missionaries provided a socially acceptable way around cherished traits without giving them up entirely since they still served functional purposes. The Hawaiians actually had a native, fermented drink, kava, but its entrenched functions, meanings, and uses militated against using it for disinhibited reduction of ten-

---

21 Rosalie Wax and Robert Thomas, "American Indians and White People," *Phylon*, XXII (1961), 305–317; A. I. Hallowell, *Culture and Experience, Selected Papers* (Philadelphia, 1955), 364–365; Ernestine Friedl, "Persistence in Chippewa Culture and Personality," *American Anthropologist*, LVIII (1956), 814–825.

22 Taking responsibility for one's own actions does not have moral connotations in terms of guilt-shame analyses of cultural compulsions to conform. Rather, it means simply a willingness to take the consequences of one's decisions—figuring things out carefully before taking action. The point is made very clearly in Wax and Thomas, "American Indians and White People," 305–317.

23 Reciprocal generosity implies that it is bad form to refuse gifts or to demonstrate a selfish desire to avoid having to give. Frances Northend Ferguson notes that this attribute has aided the program of prescribing drugs for Navaho problem drinkers in order to reduce their craving for alcohol. It is impolite to refuse the offer of a drink but the known fact that a person will get sick if he drinks while on the medicine allows him to refuse without fear of criticism from other Indians. "Navaho Drinking: Some Tentative Hypotheses," *Human Organization*, XXVII (1968), 159–167. One wonders whether the "craving" in any situation is stronger than cultural considerations.

sions about taboos.[24] Futhermore, there is nothing innate to alcohol to suggest it could or should be used for such a purpose. As the Hawaiian case illustrates, cultures do not universally deal with the need for outlets from tension with what MacAndrew and Edgerton term socially acceptable "time-out" periods of disinhibition or license. Thus, Indian drunken time-out was not an inevitable development, but it was apparently a highly expedient innovation to meet a felt need to reduce tension or perhaps replace existing methods whose nature is lost to history.[25] Innovations are always reworked to some extent to make them fit the borrowing culture; moreover, they may be continuously adapted for functional utility as the culture undergoes change.

If all this strikes the historian as far-fetched speculation, I would merely note how little attention is paid to the fact that the Indians' tobacco was as attractive to Europeans as European alcohol was to the Indians. Europeans took over smoking with only slight modifications of form and use but the religious functions and sacred meanings of smoking and tobacco itself were irrelevant and were replaced with things familiar to European thinking—the sociability and relaxed comfort of spirits in moderation, perhaps. Smoking doubtless also appealed to those who attributed sophistication to familiarity with the new things brought to Europe in the great age of discovery. Furthermore, these desires were quickly exploited by colonials seeking lucrative export crops and by home governments interested in tax revenues. The present alarming reports relating tobacco to cancer and a host of other ills have prompted Pan-Indian humorists to refer to tobacco as "the Indians' revenge"—for bringing alcohol!

Now, if Indians institutionalized patterns of drunkenness for their own internal, cultural reasons, they were encouraged by Europeans for their own, largely economic reasons. We tend to forget that there was a long period when Indian societies dealt as powerful equals with representatives of competing European groups in negotiations for trade and alliance in warfare. The Europeans needed the Indians' skills and good will as much as the Indians wanted the Europeans' trade goods. The Indians accepted and adapted vast amounts of ma-

---

24 There seems to be some disagreement whether kava can properly be defined as an alcoholic intoxicant. Cf. MacAndrew and Edgerton, *Drunken Comportment*, 42–46. On conversion in Hawaii, see Douglas Oliver, *The Pacific Islands* (Cambridge, Mass., 1952), 185.

25 See footnote 20 above, especially regarding witchcraft.

terial items from Europeans, even to completely replacing analogous native items, but they kept their own cultural, social, and political counsel as did the Europeans who were growing rich on the Indians' furs as they puffed on their pipes and haggled over prices.

The initial and continuing encounters and interactions between whites and Indians were intimately associated with alcohol. Liquor was more than a borrowed item like steel traps which became part of Indian culture. Generous distribution of liquor was soon discovered to be a good way to begin business with Indians. It augured a satisfactory contract for both parties. There was no advantage in trying to befuddle Indians in order to cheat them, at least at the beginning of contact and for a long time thereafter. The Indians could simply take their business elsewhere.[26] The fact that Indians responded somewhat differently to liquor than did whites in their extremes of drunkenness was not attributed to cultural differences. Both sides simply assumed that they were by nature constitutionally different from each other. Furthermore, for several centuries the very differences between Indian and white society were worth maintaining as each side managed what it excelled at and exchanged with the other. But, as trade declined, as international boundaries in North America were firmed up to prevent Indians from playing different white nations against each other, and as severe competition for land set in, the nature of Indian-white relationships changed. Indians still kept their own cultural, social, and political counsel but whites deemed them a nuisance with nothing to offer in exchange to justify their separate existence.

In the meantime, trade had worked changes within tribal cultures. Leaders were often elevated to greater power as they took on the roles of negotiators with whites and distributors of goods. The old pattern of the generous hunter-leader had been extended insofar as he had more to give away. With the decline of Indian power, drinking took on increasingly desperate proportions, remaining one of the last features of the good old days. Thus, Harold Hickerson observes of the Ojibwa:

---

26 Anthony Wallace, in his *Death and Rebirth of the Seneca*, 111–149, details the "play off" system employed by the Seneca (and other tribes as well) in holding a balance of power between the French and British. Although the Iroquois were particularly good at the play-off technique, it was not unique to them and was employed widely by other Indian groups in their relations with the various competing white powers: French, British, Spanish, Dutch, Mexican, American.

... brawls occurred chiefly during periods of orgiastic drunkenness in the vicinity of trading posts. Drunkenness itself was symptomatic of the decay of the old mechanisms enforcing hospitality; the distribution of liquor fell to the lot of successful trappers, perhaps at times to shamans, and this enabled them to assume the guise of "chiefs." Under the fur trade, provisions were only sporadically available for distribution; such items as venison and wild rice were traded in large amounts to the traders, and trade goods were consumed within small extended family units. The function of the distribution of liquor to be consumed communally within the band, then, was the assertion and maintenance of leadership.[27]

As the mutually advantageous features of Indian-white interaction deteriorated and Indian life became increasingly impoverished, ideals of Indian behavior became ever more difficult to sustain. Additionally, there were the pressures to give up entirely ideals of Indian behavior. Getting drunk remains a very Indian thing to do when all else fails to maintain the Indian-white boundary. It will remain so until Indian groups can achieve new, mutually satisfactory relationships with whites appropriate to contemporary opportunities.

At this point, I would like to discuss three alternatives to drinking as a means of validating Indianness. My examples are drawn from over twenty years of regular association with the Wisconsin Winnebago and four extended visits during the last ten years among the Dogrib of northern Canada. The generalized descriptions of the alternatives derive as well from briefer associations with other tribes in the Midwest, Plains, and Northwest Coast and from experiences with intertribal communities in Detroit, Chicago, and Milwaukee. The alternatives are not mutually exclusive. People who employ them may also drink, but drinking seems to be managed effectively in direct relationship to the effectiveness of the other alternatives.

An important validation of Indianness is the ability to maintain a reputation as an exemplary person in terms of basic ideals already discussed: dignity, responsibility, resourcefulness, respect for others, and reciprocal generosity. This complex is expressed in providing adequately but not conspicuously by local standards for oneself and dependents—usually a far larger group than the average white breadwinner is expected to provide for—and reasonably regular participation in activities that the community defines as Indian.

---

27 Harold Hickerson, "Ojibwa," in Eleanor Burke Leacock and Nancy Oestreich Lurie, eds., *North American Indians in Historical Perspective* (New York, 1971), 181–182.

Mountain Wolf Woman, a Winnebago friend whose autobiography has been published, operated almost entirely in terms of this first general criterion of Indianness.[28] She worked hard to provide adequately for her family which included grandchildren and great grandchildren and on occasion children of distant relatives and Indian friends who had hit on hard times. She was secure in her position in the Indian community and commanded respect as an Indian among whites. She found in the peyote religion whatever comfort she needed in times of crisis, and worked off anxieties with tears or great bursts of physical activity, such as chopping wood or house cleaning. She never drank, and expressed disapproval of drinking for its social and personal destructiveness, but she was tolerant of the drunk, firmly believing Indians were physiologically different from whites in their capacity for alcohol.

A., a middle-aged, monolingual Dogrib, is a thorough-going "bush" Indian. He works hard at fishing, trapping, hunting, and occasional wage work to support his large family which lives well by bush Dogrib standards. He engages in community activities but only recently took on a formal leadership role. He is exceedingly dignified, almost severe, in manner. However, he will join in peaceful community brew parties. When he leaves his small village to trade he makes sure that all the groceries and other family needs are provided for before sometimes treating himself to a bottle or two of rum. He finds convivial companions to share his liquor and gets hilariously drunk with them. He does not flaunt his condition or get into trouble to be picked up by the Mounties. When A. gets drunk, he does so as an exemplary Dogrib enjoying himself. He is not trying to assert Indianness. He does not need to. His drinking seems to be a socially acceptable "time-out" period from the demands of being an exemplary Dogrib without any reference to problems with white society.

A.'s brother, B., speaks a little English and is more outgoing and jovial, but not without a certain dignity of manner. He is liked in the community and considered an essentially good, hard-working man, but quite literally crazy. His nickname among the Dogrib is "White Man," partly because he likes to show off his English. But what makes him really crazy, like a white man, is that he does not drink and is

---

[28] Nancy Oestreich Lurie, ed., *Mountain Wolf Woman, Sister of Crashing Thunder* (Ann Arbor, 1961).

openly critical of those who do. B. is so thoroughly Indian otherwise in life style that the nickname is an endearment and he is considered harmlessly crazy. He is not distrusted like those educated English-speakers with steady jobs who are suspected of being sell-outs, at least potentially, to the white establishment.

Such a man is C. who, while sharing B.'s outspoken ethic about the evils of strong drink, drinks moderately if the situation warrants it. He will take a drink with Indian friends out of politeness and engages in sober social drinking with non-Indian friends. He tends to be house and possession proud, but his emulation of white standards is really part of a general orientation toward raising the community standard of living as well as his own. He sought special training and qualified as a community worker employed by the government. From a white point of view, C. would be the ideal tribal interpreter because of his objective intelligence and sophisticated grasp of English. But he is rejected by the monolingual chief and council men in favor of two far less competent and benevolently motivated men. If not entirely exemplary, their life style is clearly Indian and their relationship to whites, including in-laws in the case of one of them, is manipulative rather than cooperative or emulative. They indulge regularly in Indian drinking primarily in its recreational form but there are overtones of boundary maintenance in the case of one of the men. C. knows he is not trusted to react and interpret from a position of total Indianness, as defined by the Dogrib, in Indian-white confrontations. However, by dint of positive accomplishments in the community interest on the community's own terms, C. manages to keep up his credit as a Dogrib and finds personal security and satisfaction in being a successful innovator.

A second alternative to drinking to validate Indianness is Indian expertise. The acknowledged authority may command traditional lore and ceremonial prerogatives (or even quasi-traditional roles in revitalization movements) or the local church if it is considered the community's own institution. He may be an expert singer or dancer at powwows or an Indian guide to white sportsmen. The authority may be particularly well informed and consulted by Indians and whites about his tribe's history.

D. is a successful expert. A bilingual Dogrib in his sixties, he has a long reputation of capitalizing on his bush skills, general Indian resourcefulness, and bilingualism in relation to whites. In his younger days he carried mail, guided, and performed other tasks in which whites were dependent for their very survival on his exemplary Indianness which among the Dogrib includes tremendous physical endurance. During the last ten years he has regularly filled the role of anthropological and linguistic informant. He is respected in the Indian community as a responsible emissary, spokesman, and representative of their best qualities to the outside world. He also manages to live as well as C., the community worker, supporting his family by hunting, fishing, trapping, wage work, and foster child care. His outlook is Indian and, although he is completely at ease among whites, he always deals calculatedly, albeit in a genuinely friendly manner, with an alien people. D. enjoys well managed but properly tipsy Indian recreational drinking. His attitude is well illustrated in a recent incident when a convivial party turned into a fight during which a participant knocked out one of D.'s teeth. D. was philosophical. The fellow was drunk and did not know what he was doing and, furthermore, he was sorry enough when he sobered up to give D. five dollars by way of apology.

Another expert was the late Charles R. (Charley) Lowe Cloud, a Wisconsin Winnebago. He wrote a weekly column, "The Indian News," for the *Black River Falls Banner-Journal,* by which it achieved a national circulation among Indian cognoscenti. Although a Carlisle graduate, Charley seems to have excelled mainly in football and other sports. Since his formal education was skimpy, his broken English accounts were no put-on as sometimes alleged. A classic of journalistic brevity under his by-line once summed up the complications of his life: "Not much news this week. Indian report in jail."

Charley was frequently in jail because he was frequently drunk. The authorities would pick him up when he seemed too drunk to care for himself rather than to punish him or to imagine that they could rehabilitate him. This Charley knew and appreciated, expressing neither shame nor remorse over his bouts with the bottle. Getting drunk was something Indians did. Nor did the local Winnebago people view his drinking with anything but tolerant amusement. They were ambivalent, however, about Charley's role as newsman. They admired and quoted his outspoken criticism of the white man and approved his obvious commitment to Indian values and traditional beliefs. But they were also sometimes embarrassed by his writing insofar as it often appeared to lampoon Indians and make them appear undignified to white readers. Charley, I am sure, never realized that at times his grammar and spelling were not only funny but gave rise to unconscious *double entendres*. He was in dead earnest in his indignation and concern for the Indian community. It seemed to puzzle him that his efforts received a mixed reaction among the Winnebago but he was a man with a sense of calling and went on writing. I believe that his drinking was a desperate validation of Indianness among Indians and a classic example of exploitation, albeit probably unconscious, of Indian tolerance for the drinker. If what Charley wrote sincerely in the community interest turned out to be unintentionally offensive, Winnebago people would (and, in fact, did) forgive him since there was always the likelihood that he was not entirely sober when he took pencil in hand.

A third way of validating Indianness is what might be called leadership. I confine this definition to situations in which Indian people are in positions to promote community interests *vis à vis* white society, particularly in regard to government agencies. This is a difficult role because successful liaison efforts in communicating with whites are so easily interpreted as selling out the community or profiting at the community's expense. Yet, leaders are recognized as necessary if the Indian community is to prosper and survive at all. The successful leader usually manages both to get things done in the community behalf and to maintain personal exemplariness in Indian terms.

E. is a traditionalist Winnebago, intelligent and sensitive but with little formal education. As he approached middle-age he took on more attributes of exemplary Indianness and, as far as I know, had no reputation as a drinker when he became an active leader. He derived great satisfaction from the learning process involved in leadership and in seeing his efforts, in concert with other tribal leaders, result in material improvement for his people without in any way compromising Winnebago values. Unfortunately, as so often happens in Indian affairs, governmental agencies supplying funds for tribal work gained control of decision making and began undercutting the work accomplished by the tribe on its own initiative. E. labored to right the situation and get power back into the Winnebagos' hands but was unable to do so. He held out longer than many of his original co-workers in the new regime but finally he too resigned his office. Another Winnebago reported to me with evident approbation that E. had quit and gotten "good and drunk." Whether he did or not, it was important that people thought he did. Suspected of being a sell-out, he had redeemed himself.

F. is a mixed blood Dogrib with a history of apparent identity problems. He was a heavy drinker and might have been written off as a classic example of drinking because of a sense of status deprivation and inability to assimilate as white. He seemed to be moving in a white direction since he had taken himself off the rolls as an Indian. Canadian law has now changed, but until the early 1950s treaty Indians could not vote or buy liquor. F. may have had other motivations but the right to buy liquor often accounted for people opting out of official Indian status. A brief community development project instituted by the Canadian cooperative movement permitted F. to use his white education, bilingualism, and basically sound intelligence as a leader. Although F. had long been identified by the traditional full-blood community as a member of the "no-good" faction of mixed bloods, the efforts of the Co-op began providing employment and serving the real interests of the total community. Scarcely launched, the project was terminated by political considerations in Ottawa. Whites took over the community service contracts which the Indian Co-op needed in order to prosper. Predictably, only the small handcraft end of the Co-op's operation was allowed to remain in Indian hands, thus reinforcing the idea that Indians can only manage things that whites can recognize as "typically" Indian in the museum artifact sense. When the bids of the Indian Co-op to handle brush clearance and other community services were rejected, although the bids were sometimes lower than those of white competitors, F., who had pretty well "dried out," went back to drinking. When last seen, he was blearily insisting he was an Indian, treaty or no treaty, and indulging in the familiar expressions that he could not get ahead because he was an Indian and that he was as good as any white man. Actually, F. is one of the few Indians whose skills could assure him a good job if he wished to compete with local whites. He would suffer no personal financial loss and have greater acceptance by the white community than he had in his role as Indian Co-op leader. It is not that he drinks because he cannot get ahead in terms of white success goals; the drinking actually interferes with his getting ahead and, to me at least, seems a desperate validation of Indianness when denied the opportunity to exercise other alternatives. F. can verbalize his anger and frustration to anyone who has the patience to hear him out. The Indian community, he believes, could have handled its own affairs in its own way, namely with a co-operative, but the white government favored greedy whites whose management assured them most of the profits.

To return to my original hypothesis, I have admittedly stuck my neck out knowing I would not have space for qualifications and extensive documentation necessary to pull it back. I have only tried to make clear that I believe most studies of Indian drinking start with a mistaken assumption that it is simply *bad*. In my opinion, as an old, patterned form of recreational behavior, it is managed and probably no more hazardous to health than karate, mountain climbing, or mushroom hunting. If Indian people decide to give up recreational drinking (as it is, its intensity and frequency of occurrence vary from tribe to tribe), I am sure it will be for cultural reasons of their own, just as I believe they developed the drinking patterns initially for their own reasons. Middle-class whites concerned about Indian welfare—missionaries, social workers, psychiatrists, and others—confuse their concern for health and well-being with their embarrassment and disgust at any behavior which to them is *declassé*. Getting drunk for its own sake, like sexual promiscuity, may be fun but something "nice" people do not do, or at least do not flaunt. A persistent white, class oriented ethnocentrism prevents recognizing the otherwise exemplary, competent, "successful" Indian for what he is—an Indian doing contemporary Indian things, whether dressing decently, driving a car, or going to college. Somehow, his undignified behavior when drunk, or if he does not get drunk himself, his unwillingness to disavow or interfere strenuously with those who do, imply that he is not quite yet "just like us." The fact that Indian drinking distresses and disturbs whites and forces them to take notice may well explain why it can so easily become a form of protest, assuming my hypothesis is correct, in Indian-white encounters and can even help restore credit where one's Indian investment in the Indian community is called into question.

But protest demonstrations by definition involve extraordinary behavior and are hard to sustain indefinitely. The tragedy is that the Indian protest has been so prolonged that in some cases it becomes a way of life with disastrous consequences for the people concerned. I do not agree with Vine Deloria, Jr.'s syllogism that young Indians were sold the notion by anthropologists that Indians live in two worlds; people who live in two worlds drink; therefore, to be real Indians they must drink. But, like Deloria, I, too, have "lost some good friends who

DRANK too much." [29] Some took their lives before managing to drink themselves to death. And, like Deloria, my grief evokes anger and bitterness that they died as they did and that others are likely to go the same route so long as we pursue policies that continue to deprive Indians of lands, water rights, and other natural resources or so long as we offer them the opportunity to achieve decent living standards only if they measure up to our particular philosophical standards. [30]

The one bright ray I see at present is that Indian people are finding increasingly effective, and sober, means to express aggression and protest which are unmistakably Indian. Many Indians have turned from defensive action to offensive tactics. The last few years, for example, have witnessed the occupation of Alcatraz, the development of influential and unifying Indian publications, such as *Akwesasne Notes*, [31] the ejection of unwanted tourists from Indian land, and the successful campaign of the National Congress of American Indians to force withdrawal of a liquor ad which humorously exploited the stereotype of the drunken Indian.

---

[29] Vine Deloria, Jr., *Custer Died For Your Sins* (New York, 1970), 86. Indians were drinking long before anthropologists appeared on the scene. If they were as susceptible to the influence of the opinions of outside authorities as Deloria suggests, we would have succeeded long since in talking them out of wanting to be Indians.

[30] On November 23, 1970, the Senate Foreign Relations Committee, by a ten to two vote, finally approved a treaty outlawing genocide and sent it to the floor of the Senate. Action on the treaty, signed by many other nations, has been held up in the United States for twenty-one years. The U.P.I. dispatch appearing in papers across the country (see, e.g., *Milwaukee Journal*, Nov. 24, 1970) suggested that the delay was due to "misgivings about its effect on the court system," i.e. civil rights questions regarding blacks. If the treaty is finally ratified, it will be interesting to see whether American Indian groups will make use of it in arguing land and water rights and other issues.

[31] The editor is Jerry Gambill, Cornwall Island Reserve, Box 435, Rooseveltown, New York 13683. Appearing ten times yearly, this paper reprints news items about Indians from newspapers and magazines published throughout the United States and Canada. The emphasis is on items which describe protests against abrogation of Indians' rights.

Kiowas, Comanches, and Cattlemen, 1867-1906: A Case Study of the Failure of U.S. Reservation Policy

WILLIAM T. HAGAN

The author is a member of the history department in the State University of New York, Fredonia.

IN THE DECADE from 1865 to 1875 the United States government located most of the Plains Indians on reservations. There was almost unanimous agreement among the whites that this was the native American's best hope of survival. Friends of the Indian outdid each other in praising the reservation as an incubator in which the evolution of the primitive tribesmen might be accelerated. Yet a quarter-century later there was ample evidence that the reservation had not done the job. What had gone wrong?

Perhaps the concept had fundamental faults, but also it is true that the conditions considered necessary for success were rarely all present. One of these was isolation. There were two and a half centuries of experience to demonstrate that the Indian-white contacts that usually occurred on the frontier had damaging rather than beneficial effects on the Indians. Thus, the treaty the Kiowas and Comanches signed with the United States in 1867 not only created for them a reservation of nearly three million acres, but closed it to all white men except those on official business.[1]

The authors of this standard provision in Indian treaties could not

---

[1] Charles J. Kappler, ed., *Indian Affairs: Laws and Treaties* (5 vols., Washington, 1904), II, 977.

77

have foreseen the difficulty of enforcing it as the expanding cattlemen's frontier first lapped at the edges of the Kiowa and Comanche reservation and then swept over it. The role of the cattlemen as exploiters of Indian grazing lands and meddlers in tribal politics was an important one on many reservations, among them the Cheyenne and Arapaho, Osage, Crow, Shoshone, and Pawnee. This case study of their operations on the Kiowa and Comanche reservation should help explain why isolation proved unenforceable and why this incubator of Indian civilization failed to work as anticipated.

The Kiowa and Comanche treaty of October 21, 1867, was one of several negotiated by the Peace Commission with Plains tribes that year. By affixing their Xs to the document, the Kiowas and Comanches agreed to accept the reservation for their home and renounced their claims to other territory. For its part, the United States promised to provide certain services to the Indians and, for thirty years, an annual distribution of goods. By another treaty, the Kiowas and Comanches agreed to share their reservation with the Kiowa-Apaches, a smaller tribe that was closely associated with the Kiowas.[2]

The first tribesmen located in 1868 on their new home, but it took another seven years of military operations and delicate negotiations to persuade all of a basically nomadic people to give up their wandering ways. Equally difficult for them was the abandonment of the warfare they had carried on for years against the Texans. The Kiowas and Comanches saw nothing inconsistent in their accepting residence on their reservation, with the rations and annuities which went with such residence, while continuing to send raiding parties south of the Red River.

During the seven years which it took the Kiowas and Comanches to locate on the reservation surrounding Fort Sill, they killed scores of Texans, made captives of hundreds more, and stole thousands of horses and mules. These blows fell heaviest on the Texas cattlemen who were gradually expanding their operations west of the Cross Timbers and north to the Red River.

Two of the leaders in this movement were Samuel Burk Burnett and Daniel Waggoner, both of whom lost horses at the hands of what they called the "Fort Sill Indians."[3] Waggoner suffered the additional

---

[2] *Ibid.*, 982.

[3] Lawrie Tatum to Enoch Hoag, April 16, 1870, Office of Indian Affairs, Letters Re-

KIOWA, COMANCHE AND APACHE RESERVATION

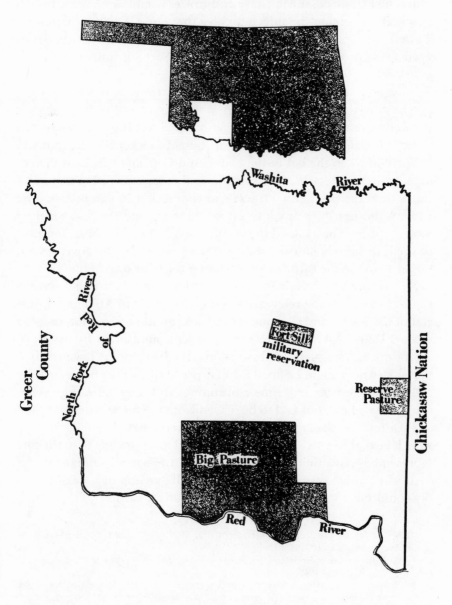

ceived, Microfilm Roll 376:862, National Archives (hereafter these rolls are cited as OIALR).

indignity of finding on the reservation, but being unable to recover, about two hundred horses he had lost. Despite the positive identification he had made, the military authorities would not risk an Indian outbreak by forcing the thieves to give them up.[4] This was hard for a Texas cattleman to take, but both Waggoner and Burnett later developed a very profitable relationship with the Fort Sill Indians and their grassland.

Waggoner and Burnett were not the first to recognize the grazing potential of the reservation. A series of military and civilian officials pointed it out and contrasted it with the difficulties of farming in western Oklahoma. In 1875 General Ranald Mackenzie, in command at Fort Sill when the last of the Kiowa and Comanche Indians surrendered, purchased for the tribesmen several thousand head of sheep and cattle from the proceeds of the sale of confiscated Indian ponies. The Indians did not show any interest in the sheep and the flocks melted away quickly. They valued the cattle more, but had to slaughter most of them to supplement the scanty rations issued by the government, rather than use the cattle as a foundation for their own herds.[5]

Meanwhile, Texans driving stock north to markets in Kansas began to intrude on the reservation. One cattle trail to Abilene ran just east of the Kiowa and Comanche land, and another, just west, pointed toward Dodge City. Sometimes by accident, most often by design of their drovers, cattle left the trails to crop the free grass. A law provided that the owners might be fined a dollar per head, but the procedure for collection was awkward, time consuming, and uncertain. The cattle could not be held, but had to be driven from the reservation and then application for damages made to a federal court. Even if the fine were levied, the owner might have obtained more grazing than the fine represented. And there were times when the agency Indian police, even when aided by soldiers from the small garrison of Fort Sill, simply could not cope with thousands of intruding cattle.[6]

---

4 Moses Wiley to the Commissioner, Sept. 25, 1870, *ibid.*, 376:1222; deposition by Daniel Waggoner, May 10, 1871, *ibid.*, 377:483.

5 P. B. Hunt to Commissioner, Dec. 31, 1878, *ibid.*, 384:656; Hunt to Commissioner, Feb. 12, 1879, *ibid.*, 384:726.

6 Hunt to Col. J. K. Mizner, May 29, 1880 (copy), *ibid.*, 386:337; Major Guy V. Henry to Assistant Adjutant General, Department of the Missouri, Feb. 28, 1882, in "Correspondence Relating to Leases of Lands in the Indian Territory," *Senate Ex. Doc. 54*, 48 Cong., 1 sess. (serial 2165), 59; Hunt to Commissioner, Dec. 31, 1883, copy in Oklahoma State Historical Society.

Individuals with contracts to supply beef for Indian agencies were also trying to obtain free pasture. The beef contractors were permitted to hold on the Indian land herds from which they would be issuing beeves to the tribesmen. Some badly abused this privilege by holding on the reservation thousands of head of cattle more than would be needed to fulfill their contracts. The excess were shipped to markets in Kansas after having grazed at no cost for several years on Kiowa and Comanche grass.[7]

The profit to be made in the cattle business if one had access to grazing that was free, or close to it, was discerned by many. Squaw men (whites married to Indian women), licensed proprietors of trading stores, even agents, tried to get in the act. The licensed traders and agents were denied permission to engage in stockraising on the side, although they may have done so surreptitiously.[8] The squaw men might be denied permission as individuals, but they could always circumvent this by operating through their Indian wives whose range rights could not be denied.[9]

The major demand for access to the grass of the Kiowa and Comanche Reservation came, however, not from the squaw men and the beef contractors. It came from the Texas cattlemen who by 1878 were beginning to hold large herds just south of Red River, and on ranches in the Chickasaw Nation just east of the reservation line. A combination of rancher greed and Indian need provided the opening wedge. Agent P. B. Hunt, who took over the administration of the agency in the spring of 1878, found the Indians in a difficult situation. The ration issued by the government was calculated on the assumption that the Indians would supplement it by hunting and farming. The Kiowas and Comanches had yet to demonstrate any capacity for farming, however, and hunting had become less and less productive as the hide hunters slaughtered the buffalo. During the winter of 1879–1880, the Indians for the first time in their history failed to make a

---

7 This practice was still going on as late as 1896. See Commissioner to Frank D. Baldwin, Oct. 17, 1896, Office of Indian Affairs, Finance Letterbook 254:16, National Archives (hereafter cited as OIA Finance LB).

8 Commissioner to Hunt, Aug. 29, 1879, Office of Indian Affairs, Land Letterbook 60:484, National Archives (hereafter cited as OIA Land LB); Commissioner to W. D. Meyers, Feb. 2, 1889, *ibid.*, 181:175.

9 For a discussion of this problem, see William T. Hagan, "Squaw Men on the Kiowa, Comanche, and Apache Reservation," in John G. Clark, ed., *The Frontier Challenge* (Lawrence, 1971), 171–202.

buffalo hunt.[10] The hide hunters had swept the herds from the plains. Hungry Indians began to seize cattle being driven across the reservation or that had drifted onto it from neighboring ranches.[11]

For the next three years the Kiowas and Comanches became the unwilling hosts to more and more cattle. A severe drought in the summer and fall of 1881 reduced the capacity of pastures south of Red River to sustain many cattle and accelerated the movement of herds onto the reservation.[12] With the limited forces at his command, agent Hunt recognized the impossibility of keeping the cattle away, and suggested leasing the range and using the proceeds to build up herds for the Indians.[13] This the Commissioner of Indian Affairs and Secretary of the Interior had difficulty in justifying legally. While they procrastinated the number of cattle munching free grass multiplied.

In the meantime, the reservation was infiltrated from a third side. That portion of Indian Territory west of the North Fork of Red River was claimed by Texas which organized it as Greer County. In 1880 and 1881 large numbers of cattle were grazing that area and were drifting east onto Indian land. One small rancher located himself on the reservation near the Greer County border and remained there undisturbed for three years, so unfrequented was the western end of the Kiowa and Comanche country.[14]

In February 1882, the Secretary of the Interior responded to the reports of agent Hunt by requesting the Secretary of War to order the commanding officer of Fort Sill, Major Guy V. Henry, to assist in the removal of Texas cattle.[15] Major Henry promised to do what he could, but observed that there were not fewer than 50,000 head of

---

10 Hunt to Commissioner, April 24, 1880, OIALR Roll 386:272.

11 Jackson and Gorham to P. B. Hunt, July 20, 1879, Kiowa Grazing File, Oklahoma State Historical Society.

12 For example, see Hunt to Commissioner, Oct. 29, 1881, in Kiowa Agency Letterbook, Oklahoma State Historical Society, Volume 10:1 (hereafter cited as KLB). Martha Buntin, "Beginning of the Leasing of the Surplus Lands on the Kiowa and Comanche Reservation," Chronicles of Oklahoma, X (1932), 369–382, is a good discussion of the problem from the agent's viewpoint.

13 "There are tens of thousands of acres," noted Hunt, "that are not touched any year, out of which a nice income might be realized." Hunt to Commissioner, Aug. 18, 1879, OIALR Roll 385:332. Hunt had previously been denied permission to run cattle on the reservation. See Hunt to Commissioner, Aug. 14, 1879, OIALR Roll 385:325, and Commissioner to Hunt, Aug. 29, 1879, OIA Land LB 60:484.

14 E. L. Clark to Hunt, July 30, 1881, Kiowa Councils File, Oklahoma State Historical Society.

15 Secretary of the Interior to Secretary of War, Feb. 1, 1882 (copy), Kiowa Grazing File.

cattle involved and he did not have enough men to do the job. The Major advised his superiors that it might be well to lease the land, as cattle would graze on it one way or the other.[16] General Philip Sheridan, commanding the Military Division of the Missouri, concurred in Major Henry's recommendation.[17]

The Major urged E. C. Sugg, a Texan who had been ranching in the Chickasaw Nation and one of those whose cattle kept drifting over the eastern boundary of the reservation, to try and lease the land.[18] Sugg did so, but, on March 4, agent Hunt peremptorily refused to agree to the lease.[19] Less than two weeks later, however, Hunt contacted Sugg and other cattlemen holding herds on the reservation and partially backed down. After conferring with the Indian chiefs and headmen, he suggested that the cattlemen supply the Indians with enough free beeves to help feed the tribesmen until July 1. In return, he would permit their cattle to remain on the reservation until that date.[20] A ration crisis had led Hunt to defy Washington policy, thus providing the cattlemen with the entering wedge for leasing.

Rising beef prices had created a deficiency in the funds available for the support of the Kiowas and Comanches as well as their neighbors, the Cheyennes and Arapahos. Despite appeals from the Indian Office, Congress had appropriated only half the $100,000 shortage; the balance was to be made up by cutting the beef rations one-quarter for the remainder of the fiscal year.[21] Hunt knew that the normal ration was inadequate and to cut it by twenty-five percent would not only be unfair but possibly productive of violence on the reservation.

Hunt responded to the crisis by asking the owners of the largest herds for the 261,000 pounds of beef he would need to provide the full ration for the remainder of the fiscal year. The cattlemen, among them E. C. Sugg, Daniel Waggoner, and Samuel B. Burnett, agreed. However, while their cattle were being turned over to the agent, Con-

---

16 Major Guy V. Henry to Assistant Adjutant General, Department of the Missouri, Feb. 28, 1882, in "Correspondence Relating to Leases of Lands," 59.

17 Acting Commissioner to Secretary of the Interior, May 19, 1882, OIA Land LB 96:89.

18 Sugg to Hunt, March 1, 1882, Kiowa Grazing File.

19 Hunt to Sugg, March 4, 1882, KLB 13:17.

20 Hunt to John Nestell, March 20, 1882, *ibid.*, 13:56-57. See also Nestell to Hunt, March 25, 27, and 31, 1882, Kiowa Grazing File; Hunt to Commissioner, April 10, 1882, KLB 10:212.

21 Commissioner to Hunt, March 15, 1882, OIA Finance LB 183:393.

gress reversed its earlier decision and restored the full ration. Prominent among those urging Congress to act was Major General John Pope, commander of the Department of the Missouri, who predicted "Indian hostilities which will lead God knows where" unless the Indians on the two reservations had their full ration restored.[22] Grudgingly, Congress took the necessary action and Hunt was so notified.

Caught by surprise, Hunt now asked for permission to issue to the Indians for breeding purposes the 340 head of cattle which had been turned over to him.[23] The Commissioner at first declined, but Hunt persisted, pointing out that the crisis at the Kiowa and Comanche Reservation had been much less serious than that at the Cheyenne and Arapahoe Reservation because he had asked for "beef instead of bayonets to keep my Indians quiet."[24] The Commissioner capitulated, but insisted that the cattlemen be required in writing to release the government "from any liability for the cattle so furnished."[25]

This conditional acceptance of the presence of the cattlemen did not presage a real change in policy. In June the Secretary of the Interior again asked the War Department's cooperation in removing the cattle which had moved onto the reservations in the western part of Indian Territory.[26] In the late summer and early fall of 1882, troops from Fort Sill and the Indian police spent weeks running off the intruding cattle.

Whether or not all the cattle had been removed by October 1882, it is apparent that within a few months the reservation again was supporting a population of thousands of non-Indian cattle. For the next two years agent Hunt reiterated to his superiors his inability to keep them off and extolled the advantages of leasing. Secretary of the Interior Henry M. Teller was difficult to convince. He opposed leasing because he believed that it would not produce a substantial return and that the presence of the cattlemen and their herds would be prejudicial to the growth of Indian stock raising.[27]

Meanwhile, the cattlemen were building fences and corrals and

---

22 Pope to Major William Drum, April 3, 1882, in *Cong. Rec.*, 47 Cong., 1 sess., 2771.
23 Annual report of Hunt, in "Annual Report of the Secretary of the Interior," *House Ex. Doc. 1*, 47 Cong., 2 sess. (serial 2100), 126.
24 Hunt to Commissioner, April 26, 1882, KLB 10:237.
25 Commissioner to Hunt, May 3, 1882, OIA Finance LB 183:591.
26 Commissioner to Hunt, June 20, 1882, OIA Land LB 98:88.
27 Teller to the Secretary of War, Aug. 5, 1882, in "Correspondence Relating to Leases of Lands," 75.

generally conducting themselves as legal occupants of the reservation. To free themselves from depredations by the real owners of the reservation, they put influential chiefs and headmen on their payrolls. The Comanches received most of this attention, their bands being generally found in the best grazing areas directly north of the Red River. Prominent among those who arrived at mutually profitable arrangements with the cattlemen was Quanah, son of a Comanche chief and a white captive, Cynthia Parker. In 1875 he had been among the last Comanches to give up his nomadic life, but once on the reservation he proved remarkably adaptable. Another friend of the cattlemen in this period was Permansu, or Comanche Jack. A nephew of the prominent chief, Ten Bears, Comanche Jack had served as a scout for the army in 1874–1875 and was currently in the Indian police. Even Isatai, the Comanche medicineman who in 1874 had inspired the attack on the buffalo hunters at Adobe Walls, had established a close relationship with a Texas cattleman.[28]

In the anti-leasing faction were most of the Kiowas. Their camps were in the northern part of the reservation, farthest from Texas and thus less attractive to the cattlemen who felt no need to cultivate Kiowa friendship. Also opposed to leasing, however, were some leading Comanches, among them Tabananaka and White Wolf, both older men and chiefs. Their disagreement with the leasing faction headed by Quanah was only one issue in the politics which divided the reservation's population into several constantly changing factions.

In the meantime, the pro-leasing forces were making headway in Washington, especially with Secretary Teller who began to think more positively on the issue. Though he could still find no legal authority for leasing, he nevertheless permitted the Indians to do so under supervision of the Department of the Interior. He insisted, however, that the number of white herders be kept to a minimum so that the Indians could be hired for this purpose, thereby providing them with jobs and permitting them to learn the rudiments of the cattle business.[29]

Although the way was now clear for leasing, the Indians were unable to reach agreement among themselves on the issue. While they

---

28 George W. Fox, Jr., to Hunt, Oct. 13, 1884, Kiowa Grazing File. According to Fox, Isatai was in his pay, while Comanche Jack was in the employ of Burnett and Waggoner, and Quanah on the payroll of a man named Groom.

29 Commissioner to Hunt, May 7, 1883, *ibid.*

bickered in council and dispatched contending delegations to Washington, the Texas cattlemen continued to pasture their herds on Indian land, and the only tribesmen to benefit were a handful of Comanches—Quanah, Comanche Jack, Isatai, and several others.[30] Agitation of the leasing issue on a number of reservations in the Indian Territory finally led to an investigation in 1884 by the Senate Committee on Indian Affairs. The Commissioner of Indian Affairs also sent his own sleuth, Special Agent Paris H. Folsom. Folsom spent over a month with the Kiowas and Comanches and concluded that a majority of them opposed leasing. He also thought he had uncovered an "Indian ring"—the descriptive term of the day for any combination of individuals who wished to defraud the Indians or the government. Folsom claimed that the ring consisted of the cattlemen agitating for the leases, agent Hunt and his chief clerk, both of whom were using their influence to further leasing, and certain Indians, Quanah in particular. He recommended strongly against approval of a proposal, made by several of the cattlemen, to lease about one and a half million acres for six cents an acre for six years. And he did so despite the fact that the cattlemen had agreed to employ fifty-four Indian herders.[31]

Agent Hunt had already forwarded a copy of the proposal with his endorsement to Washington, insisting that a majority of the adult males of the tribes had agreed to it.[32] An Indian delegation, headed by Quanah and Comanche Jack and accompanied by George W. Fox and E. C. Sugg representing the leasees, went to Washington to lobby with the Secretary of the Interior, now Lucius Q. Lamar, for the adoption of the lease.[33] Despite their entreaties, Secretary Lamar declined to ratify the "pretended lease," as he chose to describe it, but neither did he direct the agency officials to ignore it.[34] The Commissioner of Indian Affairs tried to eliminate the question of the legality of leasing by requesting the Secretary to obtain an opinion from the Attorney

---

30 In June 1884, Inspector Benedict reported 75,000 head of Texas cattle on the reservation. "Leases of Lands in the Indian Territory," *Senate Ex. Doc.* 17, 48 Cong., 2 sess. (serial 2261), 32.

31 Folsom to Commissioner, Dec. 16, 1884, in "Leases of Lands in the Indian Territory and Other Reservations," *Senate Report 1278*, 49 Cong., 1 sess. (serial 2362), 670.

32 Hunt to Commissioner, Jan. 21, 1885, *ibid.*, 763.

33 Thomas F. Woodward to Hunt, *ibid.*, 654.

34 Lamar to Commissioner, May 21, 1885, Indian Division Letterbook (hereafter cited as Indian Division LB), 40:186, National Archives; Commissioner to Hunt, May 27, 1885, OIA Land LB 137:177.

General. The Secretary did so, but he did not get a clarification of the issue. The Attorney General held that neither the President nor the Secretary of the Interior had the power to make, authorize, or approve leases of reservation lands. They could be made only by treaty or convention and would require congressional approval. However, the Attorney General concluded that, while holders of leases approved by the Indians might be ejected, they could not be punished as trespassers.[35] The issue remained unresolved and the cattlemen continued to hold herds on Indian land.

Nor could the Indians agree among themselves. Tabananaka's faction still opposed leasing, and, according to Fort Sill's commanding officer, most Kiowas and Comanches were in agreement with Tabananaka.[36] Moreover, because the anti-leasing faction had decided to refuse its share of "grass money," as the semi-annual payments of the cattlemen were known, trouble was expected.

As soon as the payments of grass money began in the summer of 1885, the government had to face the delicate question of what to do with the sums refused by the Tabananaka faction. The matter was submitted to Washington for decision by a new agent, J. Lee Hall, a former Texas Ranger who had replaced Hunt. On this sensitive matter, Secretary Lamar ruled that, although his department did not recognize any lessees on the reservation, the grass had been consumed and the Indians should get the money. Since the dissidents refused to take receipt, Hall was directed to deposit the money in their names in the United States Treasury.[37]

The first grass money payment, amounting to $27,306 or $9 per capita for those who chose to take it, had been made in July 1885 under the supervision of agent Hunt. Hall could find no record of the money expended or the amount due to those who refused payment. At the time of the second distribution, which was made in January under his direction, he found that about a third of the Indians refused to accept their shares.[38] This meant that about $20,000 was being paid out twice a year, a bonanza which for the most part ended up

---

35 Acting Commissioner to J. W. Throckmorton, Aug. 20, 1888, *ibid.*, 151:186.

36 Capt. F. W. Clous to Assistant Adjutant General, Department of the Missouri, July 14, 1885, Fort Sill Letterbooks, Microfilm copy, Manuscript Division, University of Oklahoma.

37 Lamar to the Commissioner, Dec. 19, 1885, Indian Division LB 42:380.

38 Hall to Commissioner, June 28, 1886, KLB 24:6.

in the tills of the licensed traders. Hall had another plan for it. He proposed that the money be used to purchase cows to help increase Indian herds, predicting that if this were done the Kiowas and Comanches would in three years produce more than enough beef for their own use.[39] The Commissioner of Indian Affairs refused to give his approval, however, since the leasing issue was still before Congress. "This Office can at present take no action upon your letter," he explained to Hall, "other than to file it, for future reference, should occasion arise."[40] Such a decision did not displease the traders, but neither did it contribute to Indian welfare.

A year later Hall was still urging that the grass money be used to purchase cattle, and the Commissioner and the Secretary of the Interior were still trying to disassociate themselves from any leasing arrangements.[41] Without their specific authorization, the agent continued to make deals with the cattlemen. In addition to the major contracts negotiated in December 1884, Hall had apparently approved other leases for smaller acreages. Two of these contributed to his downfall when an investigation of the agency led to charges that he had embezzled $14,008 from the grazing fund. In October 1887 he was relieved by Special Agent E. E. White.[42] Hall was acquitted of the charges, but doubts lingered about the honesty of the flamboyant Texan who is depicted by his friendly biographer as a person who went through life hoping for a stroke of fortune that would make him a wealthy man.[43]

Late in 1888 White turned the agency over to William D. Myers, who was in charge the following year when the six-year leases of 1884 came up for renewal. Quanah, the friend of the cattlemen, held out for new leases which would run for eight years. His rival, Tabananaka, preferred none, but would settle for five-year leases. They compromised at six years and the Indians in council recommended leases

39 Hall to Commissioner, Feb. 4, 1886, *ibid.*, 21:252.

40 Commissioner to Hall, March 11, 1886, OIA Land LB 145:349.

41 Commissioner to Secretary, April 2, 1887, *ibid.*, 158:118; Secretary to Commissioner, April 5, 1887, Indian Division LB 50:60.

42 Secretary to Attorney General, April 5, 1888, Indian Division LB 54:376; Secretary to Commissioner, Feb. 1, 1888, *ibid.*, 53:472.

43 Dora Neill Raymond, *Captain Lee Hall of Texas* (Norman, 1940). An ironic note to the Hall case is that Special Agent White, who expressed much righteous indignation at Hall's frailties, leased land himself. White did not run cattle on the land which he had leased, rather he sublet it and enjoyed the middleman's profit from his connections. A. J. Long to Agent, March 24, 1890, Kiowa Grazing File.

dating from February 1, 1891.[44] But anti-leasing sentiment again was on the increase in Washington.

Early in 1890 Interior Department officials once more investigated the leases.[45] Their interest had been prompted by a report to the Secretary on conditions on the Wichita, Osage, Otoe, Kaw, and Kiowa and Comanche reservations. According to the report, any attempt to introduce allotments in severalty would be hampered by the grazing leases found on the reservations. So long as such arrangements provided the Indians with a cash income, they could be expected to resist allotment. The Secretary and the Commissioner responded by ordering that no more cattle be permitted on the reservations and that those already present be removed by October 1, 1890. They admitted that "this plan will not be without its embarrassment and difficulties," [46] but there was some urgency in the matter since on February 17 a presidential proclamation had ordered the removal of all non-Indian stock from the Cherokee Strip. Officials feared that some of this stock would show up on neighboring reservations.

For the next two years the leasing question was the principal issue on the reservation. As soon as the cattlemen learned of the October 1, 1890, deadline, they agitated successfully for a two-month extension.[47] Then, on the grounds that the government had violated the lease agreement, they refused to make the last semi-annual grass money payment. Some of them also began to remove the wire fences which, according to the leases, were to revert to the Indians.[48] In addition, they displayed their usual reluctance to comply with orders to vacate the reservation, and, when they did, they demonstrated the familiar inability to keep the cattle from recrossing the Red River or the eastern reservation line. Agent Adams, like his predecessors, protested constantly about his impotence to enforce the ban on non-Indian

---

44 E. L. Clark to Agent, Aug. 2, 1889, Kiowa Grazing File. Tabananaka's role as spokesman for the anti-leasing faction was being taken over by a Kiowa, Lone Wolf. This is not the raider who was imprisoned in the 1870s, but rather his foster son who assumed the name when the first Lone Wolf died in 1879.

45 Secretary to Commissioner, Feb. 28, 1890, Indian Division LB 64:29; Commissioner to Secretary, March 13, 1890, OIA Land LB 195:323; Secretary to Commissioner, March 19, 1890, Indian Division LB 64:165.

46 Acting Commissioner to Secretary, March 28, 1890, OIA Land LB 196:275.

47 Commissioner to Secretary, Oct. 24, 1890, *ibid.*, 206:102.

48 John Charlton to Merrill E. Gates, Dec. 15, 1890, in "Annual Report of the Secretary of the Interior," *House Ex. Doc. 1*, 51 Cong., 2 sess. (serial 2841), 807.

stock. Six months after the December deadline, there still were 75,000 to 125,000 head of cattle illegally on the reservation. According to an Interior Department inspector, some of the chiefs and headmen were being paid by the cattlemen to keep quiet. The inspector also questioned the honesty of Adams and some of his employees, particularly the chief clerk who had accepted from cattlemen a railroad pass good for a thousand miles.[49]

After securing assurances of cooperation from the War Department, the acting Commissioner of Indian Affairs ordered agent Adams to obtain troops from Fort Sill and to clear the reservation of the intruding cattle.[50] Once again cavalrymen and Indian police moved herds south of the Red River and east of the reservation line. Before they returned to Fort Sill and the agency headquarters, however, the herds had begun to drift back. Complicating the problem was the fact that some of the leading Kiowas and Comanches continued to accept beeves and money from the cattlemen. For example, Daniel Waggoner's cowboys used such bribes to gain access to a thousand square miles of pasture, and other cattlemen operated as usual at their old stands.[51]

The Texans also benefitted from a decline in the anti-leasing faction of Indians. A break apparently occurred when these Indians learned that they were eligible for over $50,000 in back grass money which had accumulated because of their earlier refusal to accept their shares. Tempted by the prospect of receiving such a large sum, many dissidents, including Lone Wolf of the Kiowas, began urging the negotiation of new leases.[52] This became apparent in March 1892, when Lone Wolf represented the Kiowas in a delegation to Washington. Also in the delegation were Quanah who spoke for the Comanches, White Man who represented the Kiowa-Apaches, George D. Day, the new reservation agent, and Colonel W. W. Flood, an attorney whose retainers included the cattlemen, Daniel Waggoner and Samuel B.

---

49 Inspector Arthur W. Tinker to Secretary, June 30, 1891, OIA Letters Received, 26273-1891.

50 Lt. A. G. C. Quay to Post Adjutant, Oct. 3, 1891 (copy), Kiowa Grazing File; Commissioner to Secretary, Oct. 20, 1891, OIA Land LB 224:238.

51 W. F. Harn to Commissioner of the General Land Office, March 7, 1892, Special Case 191, Office of Indian Affairs, National Archives. Special Case 191 consists of about fifty trays of documents, arranged chronologically which relate to grazing and agricultural leases on the Kiowa and Comanche Reservation.

52 C. E. Adams to Commissioner, Feb. 20, 1890, KLB 32:297; Council Resolution of May 26, 1890, OIA Letters Received, 17186-1890.

Burnett.[53] According to a newspaper account, the cattlemen had paid the expenses of the delegation for the express purpose of obtaining new leases.[54]

Faced with the combination of cattlemen, Indians, and the agent, Interior Department officials changed course. Also encouraging their shift in attitude was a law passed by Congress in February 1891 which legitimitized grazing leases for periods not exceeding five years.[55] Even so, the Secretary limited leases on the Kiowa and Comanche reservation to one year.[56] Following the government's action, the Indians met in council in the spring of 1892 and approved five leases for 1,300,000 acres at a rate which could not be less than six cents per acre. The lessees were the "Big Five": E. C. Sugg, C. T. Herring, Samuel B. Burnett, Daniel Waggoner, and J. P. Addington, cattlemen with a long history of association with the reservation.[57] Six additional leases for nearly 250,000 acres were also negotiated. The Secretary insisted that these leases be negotiated only after the Indians had advertised for the highest bidder. The Indians opposed open bidding, claiming that they preferred to deal with people whom they knew rather than with strangers.[58] As it turned out, the advertising for bids resulted in a reduction in income for the Indians. Instead of the six cents per acre which they had been prepared to pay, they were forced to accept bids which averaged only about five cents an acre for the six tracts.[59]

Although the Indians lost a little money because of the department's insistence on advertising, they also benefited from a small windfall. The Big Five paid $19,000 as compensation for the semi-annual payment which they had not made on the previous six-year leases. That sum was paid at the same time as the $54,000 in other grass money payments which had been refused over the years. The total of nearly $75,000 was used by the Indians to purchase wagons as well as lumber for new homes.[60] A Kiowa calendar history memorialized the payment

53 L. T. Miller to Secretary, March 14, 1892, Special Case 191.

54 G. B. Stone to Secretary, March 16, 1892, *ibid.*

55 *U.S. Statutes at Large*, XXVI, 794.

56 Secretary to Commissioner, April 21, 1892, Indian Division LB 75:270; Commissioner to Agent G. D. Day, April 25, 1892, OIA Land LB 236:115.

57 Proceedings of a Council at the Kiowa Agency, May 5, 1892, Kiowa Grazing File.

58 Petition to Secretary and Commissioner, June 7, 1892, Special Case 191.

59 Acting Secretary to Commissioner, Feb. 20, 1893, *ibid.*

60 "Annual Report of the Secretary of the Interior," *House Ex. Doc. 1*, 52 Cong., 2 sess. (serial 3088), 385.

with a row of circles to represent the silver dollars in which the Indians were paid.[61]

The Kiowa calendar history did not record another event that year which ultimately would have a shattering impact on all the residents of the reservation. In the fall of 1892 the Kiowas and Comanches were visited by the Cherokee Commission headed by David Jerome. The Dawes Severalty Act of 1887 had not applied to the Indians of Oklahoma, so two years later Congress had passed a law applying directly to them. The Cherokee Commission created for this purpose spent three weeks on the reservation in the fall of 1892 and, when negotiations had ended, the two sides had agreed to the so-called Jerome Agreement.[62] It provided that a 160-acre farm be allotted to each Indian and that the surplus land be made available to the general public. As this would put an end to their use of the reservation's grass, the cattlemen opposed congressional ratification of the agreement. Their opposition was one factor in delaying its implementation for a decade. A month after the Cherokee Commission left the reservation, Quanah was in Washington with agent Day lobbying for renewal of the leases for the Big Five.[63]

For the next six years the annual battle of the leases was fought and with the same outcome each year—renewal at six cents per acre. Divisions within the Indian ranks persisted, but there was little opposition to leasing. Instead the Indians quarreled about the distribution of the proceeds. Many were angered because of the special gifts which some of their leaders continued to receive from the cattlemen. Quanah was the principal target for this criticism, and it is obvious that the cattlemen had not forgotten him. An engraved .45 caliber revolver, a diamond stick pin, and junkets to Fort Worth, Dallas, and Washington, D.C., were some of his more easily detectable rewards. On one occasion he admitted receiving money, but he claimed that it was in exchange for his protection of the herds from the depredations of other Indians and had nothing to do with grass money.[64] Quanah was not alone. Lone Wolf, the most prominent Kiowa of this period, and White Wolf, a Comanche chief and a bitter critic of Quanah, were

---

[61] James Mooney, "Calendar History of the Kiowa Indians," in *Seventeenth Annual Report of the Bureau of American Ethnology* (Washington, 1898), 364.

[62] Transcript of Jerome Commission Proceedings at Fort Sill and Anadarko, in "Kiowa, Comanche, and Apache Indian Reservation," *Senate Doc. 77*, 55 Cong., 3 sess. (serial 3731), 8–57.

[63] Commissioner to Secretary, Dec. 3, 1892, OIA Land LB 248:368.

[64] Council with the Commissioner, March 17, 1898, OIA Letters Received, 12521½-1898.

also on the payroll of cattlemen.[65] Undoubtedly other chiefs and headmen were on someone's payroll.

With tribal leaders now finding it profitable to support leasing, the burden of opposing such arrangements was assumed by others. The Jerome Agreement had created a new interest group, those who hoped to see the reservation "opened," to use the contemporary expression for allotment and the sale of the surplus lands. Potential settlers clamored for the opportunity to homestead 160-acre farms and they were loudly supported by businessmen in the small towns neighboring the Indian land. Merchants envisioned their communities booming with the trade from the thousands of settlers who would flock to the area following the opening of the reservation. Both the businessmen and the hopeful settlers identified the big cattlemen as the villains in the long delay in ratifying the Jerome Agreement. The columns of the Minco *Minstrel*, the Marlo *Magnet*, and the Chickasha *Express* rang with denunciations of "cattle syndicates," "paid boodle gang," and "rich cattlemen." The newspapers reported on numerous mass meetings in the fall of 1893 which were designed to speed the opening of the "Fort Sill Country."[66]

In Congress, Oklahoma Territory Delegate Dennis Flynn pushed for the opening, but he was opposed successfully by members of the Texas congressional delegation, among them Representative Joseph Bailey, alleged to be an attorney for the cattlemen. Nor did the Texans neglect opportunities to cultivate the executive branch. One came their way in the spring of 1894 in the person of Colonel J. D. Cobb of Georgia, a cousin of Secretary of the Interior Hoke Smith. Cobb apparently convinced the Big Five that he could help them to retain the six-cent per acre rate and even to extend the time period from one to three years. A contract signed by Samuel B. Burnett and witnessed by Daniel Waggoner would have paid the good colonel $2,878.67 (one cent per acre on 287,867 acres) on the day that Burnett's lease was renewed on the specified terms. There is no evidence that Cobb ever delivered or that Burnett paid a cent, but the example indicates how far the cattlemen were prepared to go to retain their lucrative leases.[67]

---

65 Wilson and Silberstein to Agent Frank D. Baldwin, June 25, 1896, Kiowa Grazing File; deposition of J. N. Jones, April 28, 1899, *ibid.*

66 Minco *Minstrel*, Oct. 14, 1893, p. 2; Guthrie *Daily Leader*, Nov. 2, 1893, p. 2; Chickasha *Express*, Nov. 10, 1893, p. 1; Marlow *Magnet*, Nov. 30, 1893, p. 1.

67 Trying to confirm the story, Agent Frank D. Baldwin wrote to six cattlemen. KLB 49:161–66; see also Baldwin to Secretary, Jan. 28, 1896, Special Case 191.

The Indians were also becoming more sophisticated in their lobbying techniques. In the spring of 1893 they hired W. C. Shelley, a former employee of the Indian Bureau, to defend them against claims filed by settlers for losses to Indian raiding parties in the period 1850–1880. Shelley's career as attorney for the Kiowas and Comanches was complicated by the fact that he also accepted as clients some traders, who had alienated the Indians by sharp practices, and squaw men, whose holdings of 200,000 acres of pasture land had aroused jealousy and suspicion.[68] Nevertheless, Shelley had introduced a resolution into Congress calling for a ten-cent per acre rate.[69] Though it failed to pass, cattlemen were worried. They became especially concerned when federal officials told them that February 1898 was the deadline for bids on new leases—leases that would run for only three years and for which the minimum bid would be ten cents per acre.[70] The cattlemen put up an energetic though brief resistance to the new rate. Samuel Burnett wrote a long letter to the Secretary arguing that he could not pay ten cents an acre and remain in business. He and others also subsidized a trip to Washington by Quanah and other Indians who protested to the Commissioner of Indian Affairs.[71] The Commissioner defended the higher rate and told the Indians that the cattlemen protested only because they were unable to pay the additional four cents an acre while at the same time making special payments to the chiefs.[72] Faced with the adamant refusal of Washington officials to capitulate, the cattlemen gave in and negotiated the new leases, nearly all of which were for three years. Twenty-three leases were contracted and they provided the Indians with nearly $190,000 a year. Significantly, however, about sixty-five percent of the acreage went to only three men, E. C. Sugg, Samuel B. Burnett, and William T. (Tom) Waggoner, the son of Daniel Waggoner.[73]

---

68 Although their combined landholdings were less than those of a Burnett, a Waggoner, or a Sugg, the squaw men were a force in reservation politics equal to the cattlemen.

69 W. C. Shelley to Secretary, March 15, 1898, OIA Letters Received, 12555-1898.

70 Secretary to Commissioner, March 16, 1898, Indian Division LB 94:383.

71 Burnett to Secretary, March 11, 1898, Special Case 191; W. C. Shelley to Secretary, March 15, 1898, OIA Letters Received, 12555-1898.

72 Council with the Commissioner, March 17, 1898, *ibid.*, 12521½-1898.

73 "Annual Report of the Secretary of the Interior, 1898," *House Ex. Doc. 5*, 56 Cong., 1 sess. (serial 3915), xxxiii; abstract of leases on Kiowa and Comanche reservation, Special Case 191.

In the meantime, the Indians became more interested than ever in leasing reservation land. This was prompted largely by the expiration of the annuity provisions in the 1867 treaty and the resulting need for revenue by the Indians.[74] The Indian Bureau gave strong tacit support to the new drive since it feared that the cutoff of rations would increase Indian opposition to the Jerome Agreement. A special agent reporting to the Commissioner and an inspector operating out of the Secretary of the Interior's office urged the leasing of tracts heretofore not sought by cattlemen. They felt justified in making their recommendation because of the boom in the cattle business during the spring and summer of 1898—a boom which suggested that it would be easy to find customers for an additional 500,000 acres of pasture. Convinced by their arguments, the Commissioner in November 1898 ordered his agent on the reservation to seek bids on additional leases which would run for two years beginning on April 1, 1899.[75] An Indian council quickly ratified the decision and within a few months the land under lease increased to 2,183,953 acres and the income to the tribesmen to $216,308.15 per year, or about $70 per capita.[76] But this was high tide for the cattlemen, the squaw men, and the few Indians able to take advantage of the economic opportunities available to them. The Jerome Agreement, the legality of which the Indians had been protesting since 1892, became law on June 6, 1900.[77]

The document which Congress wrote into law in 1900 was not exactly like the one which the Jerome commission took to Washington in 1892. One innovation provided for a 480,000-acre tract which was to be held in common by the Indians. Nevertheless, most of the reservation was allotted to the tribesmen or opened to the public for settlement. This development worried the cattlemen. Heretofore they had been using two-thirds of the reservation and now they would be reduced to using less than one-seventh of it. But there was even uncertainty about this. As usual the Indians did not agree on what should

---

74 Some rations were still issued to school children, police, and those physically incapacitated.

75 Acting Commissioner to Secretary, March 4, 1898, OIA Land LB 187:292; Special Agent Joseph Pray to Commissioner, Sept. 3, 1898, Special Case 191; Inspector Cyrus Beede to Secretary, Sept. 15 and 19, 1898, *ibid.*; Acting Commissioner to Agent Walker, Nov. 15, 1898, Kiowa Grazing File.

76 Proceedings of a Council at the Kiowa Agency, Nov. 19, 1898, Special Case 191; Commissioner to Secretary, Dec. 23, 1899, OIA Land LB 213:87.

77 *U.S. Statutes at Large*, XXXI, 676.

be done with the land. One group advocated dividing the 480,000 acres and thereby increasing the allotment of individual Indians.[78] Most desired to hold it in common, however, so that they might continue to derive some income from leases. Their current agent, Colonel James D. Randlett, a retired army officer and a good administrator, proposed a plan which won approval in Washington. He divided the 480,000 acres into four grazing areas, the largest of which, Big Pasture, fronted on the Red River and consisted of 414,300 acres. Randlett rented it to cattlemen. The other three pastures were located in various parts of the reservation and used for Indian stock, though any surplus in these grazing reserves was leased. As the Comanches had the most cattle, two of the pastures were located near the area they had always occupied, while the other was situated further north where it could be used by the Kiowas and Kiowa-Apaches.[79]

Once the location of the grazing reserves was known, there were prompt cries of outrage from the town of Duncan, which lay on the eastern boundary of the reservation and which would be immediately adjacent to a 22,500-acre pasture.[80] The prospect of having range land with a population of cattle to the west of the community, instead of farms occupied by potential customers, drove the Duncanites into a frenzy. The pressure they generated resulted in the pasture being made available for agricultural leases, further reducing the acreage available to cattlemen.

The Big Pasture was also the object of a bitter struggle. Randlett subdivided it into four pastures, each of which was leased at ten cents per acre to Texans who had been on the reservation for years. Sugg, Burnett, and Tom Waggoner signed three of the leases. The fourth went to Asher Silberstein, another Texan who had been leasing reservation land for several years.[81] With the possible exception of Silberstein, no one was happy with this arrangement. Each could point to corrals, tanks, fences, and bunkhouses which he had constructed and maintained but was now forced to give up. Equally disconcerting was

[78] Minutes of council of Indians with Agent Randlett, in Box 1, C. Ross Hume Collection, University of Oklahoma Manuscript Division.

[79] Randlett to Commissioner, March 1, 1901, KLB 281; Randlett to Commissioner, April 13, 1901 (copy), Box 361693, Fort Worth Federal Records Center; Randlett to Commissioner, June 3, 1901, Special Case 191.

[80] Alexander Gullett and W. I. Gilbert to Randlett, June 6, 1901, Kiowa Grazing File.

[81] Randlett to Commissioner, Oct. 15, 1901, KLB 92:201.

the influx of thousands of land-hungry "sooners" trying to get a jump on their competition. Claiming the right to move freely on public roads through the reservations, they swarmed through the leased pastures setting grass fires and disturbing the cattle. The final blow to Sugg, Burnett, and Waggoner was the sight of their fellow Texans pushing herds across the Red River and occupying illegally the pastures which the three had once leased. Tom Waggoner damned them as "little cattle men that has no right whatever there" and who had dared "forbid me watering my cattle in my tanks."[82] His righteous indignation had ironical overtones; his father, thirty years earlier, had located his stolen horses in an Indian camp and then been unable to recover them.

Sugg and Burnett took out their frustrations on each other. Since Sugg's new pasture had been carved largely from Burnett's old lease, Burnett did his best to prevent Sugg's men from constructing the necessary fences. The major battle was fought in Washington, however. Both Texans went there and enlisted help where they could find it. Sugg was aided by Representative Charles Curtis of Kansas and by an attorney for the Chicago, Rock Island and Pacific Railroad.[83] But Burnett brought up even heavier artillery in the person of Joseph Bailey, now a Texas senator, who accompanied him on a visit to the Commissioner of Indian Affairs. He was also helped by a congressman who interceded for him with the Secretary of the Interior.[84] Agent Randlett, a stern old man used to having his own way, protested when Burnett went over his head and expressed "sorrow and shame because of the degradation to which I have been subjected."[85] But Burnett succeeded in holding onto most of the disputed land until the leases expired on March 31, 1902.

Colonel Randlett was not a man to trifle with, however. In an attempt to increase profits for the Indians, he further subdivided the Big Pasture so that more cattlemen could bid for leases. In addition,

---

82 Waggoner's piteous "I have no chance to do any thing only starve to death" would have carried more weight had the Waggoner family not been one the wealthiest in Texas. Waggoner to Randlett, Sept. 11, 1901, Special Case 191.

83 Curtis to Commissioner, June 28, 1901, *ibid.*; M. A. Low to Commissioner, Nov. 9, 1901, *ibid.*

84 Burnett to Commissioner, Dec. 16, 1901, *ibid.*; Burnett to Hon. W. P. Brownlow, Aug. 31, 1901, *ibid.*

85 Randlett to Sugg, Nov. 2, 1901, KLB 92:318; Randlett to Commissioner, Nov. 11, 1901, *ibid.*, 92:343.

he successfully opposed Senator Bailey's attempt, supported by eleven other members of the Texas delegation, to extend for five months the existing leases.[86] The new leases, which ran for three years beginning July 1, 1902, required Burnett and Waggoner to pay an average of nearly thirty cents an acre. That they were prepared to do so, despite their piteous cries of distress, suggests what a fine bargain the Kiowa and Comanche grass had been for them during the earlier years. For the Indians the new leases meant annual grass payments of over $130,000.[87]

During the life of the new leases, settlers in Texas and Oklahoma Territory lobbied for the opening of the 480,000 acres. Pressing the issue in Washington were Representative James J. Stephens from Vernon, Texas, a community which stood to profit by the replacement of cows by settlers in the Big Pasture,[88] and Delegate Bird S. McGuire of Oklahoma Territory. Agent Randlett gave partial support to the move. He recommended the opening of only that portion of the 480,-000 acres which would remain after the Indian children born since June 1, 1901, had been allotted 160-acre homesteads.[89] This represented a compromise for Randlett. Like the agents who had preceded him, he recognized that, while agricultural leases meant higher income for the Indians, they also violated the isolation concept by introducing large numbers of whites among the Indians. Within a year Congress had enacted a measure similar to that urged by Randlett. It allotted land to the Indian children born since 1901 and opened the remainder of the 480,000 acres to settlement.[90] The legislation prepared the way for the passing of the cattlemen's era, which formally ended with the expiration of the last leases on July 1, 1905.

As the last steers were driven from the Big Pasture, a quarter-century's association of the Texas cattlemen with the Kiowa and Co-

---

86 Randlett to Commissioner, Nov. 12, 1901, Special Case 191; Commissioner to Secretary, Feb. 8, 1902, OIA Land LB 520:204; telegram from Randlett to Commissioner, Feb. 22, 1902, Special Case 191; telegram from Randlett to Commissioner, Feb. 24, 1902, KLB 97:127; memorials by Texas senators and congressmen, Special Case 191.

87 Acting Secretary to Commissioner, May 21, 1902, Special Case 191; *Annual Report of the Department of the Interior, 1902* (Washington, 1903), 290.

88 In arguing for his bill, Stephens claimed that opening the land would provide the Indians with revenue which would free them from dependence on the government. *Cong. Rec.*, 57 Cong., 2 sess., 2290. See also John Curry Haley, "The Opening of the Kiowa and Comanche Country" (M. A. thesis, University of Oklahoma, 1940), 104–105.

89 Randlett to Commissioner, June 14, 1905, KLB 118:402.

90 34 *U.S. Stat.*, 213.

manche Indians was over. It had extended through most of the life of
the reservation itself. For the cattlemen it had been a very profitable
association, providing them at the peak of their operations with access
to two million acres of range land at bargain rates. For the Indians the
relationship provided about $2,000,000 in grass money between 1885
and 1906. Moreover, influential chiefs and headmen received additional thousands of dollars for their good offices. Nor should it be forgotten that the cattlemen formed a powerful lobby against ratification
of the Jerome Agreement and that they helped delay the opening of
the reservation for several years.[91]

But for the Indians the relationship was more harmful than good.
Most of the grass money was expended frivolously as the Indians surrendered to the impulse to satisfy immediate urges and did little to
improve their long term economic condition. Indian service personnel
were equally culpable due to their initial reluctance to assume responsibility for leases and the income they produced. And the extra
funds which Quanah and his colleagues received corrupted leadership
when the Indians desperately needed it. Disagreements over policy
and revenue contributed to tribal factionalism, particularly among
the Comanches who were always more band than tribe oriented. Nor
could agents, whose tenure in the 1880s and 1890s averaged only about
two years, brush aside cattlemen like Burnett, Waggoner, and Sugg
who had been on the reservation since the early 1880s and had powerful friends there and in Washington. Finally, the isolation believed so
necessary during the reservation period was irrevocably shattered as
the cattlemen and their cowboys invaded the sanctuaries. Their success encouraged emulation, as in the case of the small operator who
announced that he was tired of paying pasture rent and was marrying
an Indian girl in order to enjoy free grass as a squaw man.[92]

Final blame must rest on Congress and ultimately on the people of
the United States, however. The reservation system would have func-
tioned better if Americans had been prepared to subsidize the experi-
ment properly. If they had, the Kiowas and Comanches would not
have had to sell their grass to supplement their rations and annuities,
thereby opening the door to the influx of cattlemen and their stock.

91 Donald J. Berthrong believes that the absence of a cattleman's lobby on the
Cheyenne–Arapaho Reservation helps explain why those Indians were allotted land
earlier than the Kiowas and Comanches. See Berthrong's "Cattlemen on the Cheyenne–
Arapaho Reservation, 1883-1885," *Arizona and the West*, XIII (1971), 5-32.
92 Baldwin to Commissioner, Aug. 3, 1897, KLB 55:357.

The Political Context
of a New Indian History

ROBERT F. BERKHOFER, JR.

The author is professor of history in the University of Wisconsin.

POLITICAL AGITATION outside the academy and disciplinary trends within point to a new focus for American Indian history. White politicians and other Americans discovered the "New Indians" and "Red Power" only shortly after social scientists became aware of "Pan-Indianism" and the "Urban Indian." People learned that Indians rather than having disappeared through extermination or assimilation number more today than they have for perhaps a century and a half and that their representatives employ new techniques to assert old demands. To some scholars all this appeared to be nothing short of a "renascence" in Indian life and affairs.[1] In line with these trends, the great desideratum in writing Indian history becomes putting more of the Indians into it. In short, American Indian history must move from being primarily a record of white-Indian relations to become the story of Indians in the United States (or North America) over time.

As clear as the demand for a new Indian history is the need for some new focus to meet that demand. Such a new focus would seem to be offered in the very theme of ethnic survival and cultural continuity and change. If white assumptions about racial superiority and the

---

1 See particularly Nancy O. Lurie, "An American Indian Renascence?," in Stuart G. Levine and Nancy O. Lurie, eds., *The American Indian Today* (Deland, Fla., 1968), 187-208. For the use of the terms, "New Indians" and "Red Power," consult Stanley Steiner, *The New Indians* (New York, 1968). Two brief summaries of Pan-Indianism are Robert K. Thomas, "Pan-Indianism," in Levine and Lurie cited above, and William W. Newcomb, Jr., "A Note on Cherokee-Delaware Pan-Indianism," *American Anthropologist*, LVII (1955), 1041-1045. A bibliography on the urban Indian has been compiled by Professor William H. Hodge of the Department of Anthropology, University of Wisconsin-Milwaukee, mimeo., Oct. 1968.

multifarious activities that this belief took in relation to Indian societies provide the basic theme of a history of white-Indian relations,
then the central theme of a new history of Indians ought to be the
remarkable persistence of cultural and personality traits and ethnic
identity in Indian societies in the face of white conquest and efforts at
elimination or assimilation. By concentrating on this latter theme, the
historian moves Indian actors to the center of the stage and makes
Indian-Indian relations as important as white-Indian ones have been
previously. In fact, such a theme not only transforms the chief subject
of attention but also broadens the spatial and temporal limits of the
story to a time before white contact and beyond the reservation of
yesterday to the urban ghetto and national Indian organizations of
today.[2]

The problem is how to achieve this aim. If the task of the new Indian history is to get from an aboriginal past to an urban and national
present, then it would seem appropriate for the historian to look to
the anthropologist for aid on the two ends of the time spectrum. After
all, anthropologists reconstruct the aboriginal social and cultural life
of Indian tribes, and they have also become interested recently in the
urban Indian as well as the full range of reservation Indian life. Cooperation between the historian and the anthropologist, which once
only seemed desirable in the recording of white-Indian relations, now
appears necessary to the writing of a new Indian history with its
changed focus. But the more the historian turns for help to anthropology, the more he must share some of the theoretical dilemmas beset-
ting that discipline. To make persistence and change and Indian-
Indian relations the chief subjects of a new Indian history introduces
difficulties of evidence and theory not heretofore faced squarely by
either historians or anthropologists. The major dilemma concerns the
reconciliation of the two obvious but seemingly contradictory facts
presumed basic to Indian life: Indian societies and ways of life
changed drastically over the years at the same time that Indian ethnic

---

[2] The preface to Edward H. Spicer, *A Short History of the Indians of the United
States* (New York, 1969), 3–4, presents a good brief statement of what a new focus means.
I believe the focus proposed in this article meets the demand made by Bernard W.
Sheehan, "Indian-White Relations in Early America: A Review Essay," *William and
Mary Quarterly*, XXV (1969), 267–286, for a more dynamic Indian history. Pertinent
to the theme of persistence and change is Nancy O. Lurie, "The Enduring Indian,"
Natural History, LXXV (Nov. 1966), 10–22.

identities and societies remained static and elements of personality and culture are said to have persisted unchanged.

So perplexing and so fundamental is this dilemma in interpreting Indian studies that the disciplines of history and anthropology long took different sides rather than attempting the necessary reconciliation. Anthropologists studied the aboriginal past and reservation present, while historians devoted themselves to the period in between. Anthropologists stressed the persistence of aboriginal social and cultural patterns and even basic personality into the present while historians emphasized the fundamental changes wrought in Indian life by white government policy and military might. Even in sources and subject matter the two disciplines differed as a result of their positions on the dilemma of persistence and change. Anthropologists used evidence gathered in the field from live informants, for their assumptions about cultural persistence justified the use of present-day information to describe past events. Historians, on the other hand, went to the library in search of books and manuscripts because they believed that change invalidated any evidence but that derived contemporaneously to the event studied. Historians, therefore, generally treated Indian history as a record of Indian-white relations regardless of whose "side" they considered morally correct.[3] When anthropologists looked at the history of a tribe, it was in terms of acculturation. Even then they stressed the enduring elements of the society and culture in the midst of change, preferably in value-free terms. For historians, whites were the main actors; for anthropologists, the Indian culture or society was the center of attention. In both cases, the story of the concrete dynamics and the specific Indian actors was usually omitted. Furthermore, both disciplines presumed the irreversible trend of Indian disappearance through assimilation, whether in acculturation study or in history. Indian history in this view moved implicitly, if not explicitly, in linear progression from noble or ignoble savage to reservation ward, to marginal man, and to eventual assimilation.[4]

---

3 For example, Randolph C. Downes, *Council Fires on the Upper Ohio: A Narrative of Indian Affairs in the Upper Ohio Valley Until 1795* (Pittsburgh, 1940), professes to see affairs from the Indian view but really tells the story of white diplomacy.

4 The basic division between the two disciplines may be seen in the type of textbooks common to each. In spite of its title, the comprehensive little history by William T. Hagan, *American Indians* (Chicago, 1961), concentrates upon the story of white-Indian relations. The standard anthropological texts on North American Indians present generally an atemporal view of aboriginal cultures: Ruth Underhill, *Red Man's Amer-*

The obviously complementary positions of each discipline led scholars in both to attempt a marriage of interests in the early 1950s in the name of ethnohistory.[5] What appeared to be a marriage then now looks more like a courtship, for the two disciplines still remain apart in their approaches and perspective upon Indian studies. On the whole, anthropologists have utilized historical documentary sources in their ethnological reconstructions and acculturation studies more than historians have added anthropological theory or ethnological data to their approaches to Indian history.[6] More significant than either the courtship or supposed marriage and subsequent alienation of affections are the implications of the anthropological studies of the past two decades—studies based on the broadened perspective for the writing of a new Indian history.

At the same time as anthropologists in ethnological and acculturation studies lessened the cleavage between history and their own discipline by use of documentary sources, they increased the problems connected with the basic dilemma of persistence and change. Closer attention to historical events, combined with observation of urban and rural Indians as well as the entire range of ideas and behavior on and off reservations, led many anthropologists to question previously held truths about persistence and change. Much that was once simply

---

ica: A History of Indians in the United States (1st ed., Chicago, 1953); Robert F. Spencer, Jesse D. Jennings, et al., The Native Americans: Prehistory and Ethnology of the North American Indians (New York, 1965); Wendell Oswalt, This Land Was Theirs: A Study of the North American Indians (New York, 1966). The same point is made by Murray L. Wax, "The Whiteman's Burdensome 'Business': A Review Essay on the Change and Constancy of Literature on the American Indians," Social Problems, XVI (1968), 106–113.

[5] An early proponent of such cooperation, William N. Fenton, states his case in "Indian and White Relations in Eastern North America: A Common Ground for History and Ethnology," in Fenton et al., American Indian and White Relations to 1830: Needs and Opportunities for Study (Chapel Hill, 1957), 3–27. The formation and background of the Ohio Valley Historic Indian Conference, forerunner of the present-day American Society for Ethnohistory, is briefly treated in the short first issue of its journal, Ethnohistory (1954). Subsequent symposia on the nature of ethnohistory are in ibid., VIII (Winter 1961), 12–92; XIII (Winter-Spring 1966), 1–85.

[6] I base this statement upon my impression of the declining percentage of historians vis-à-vis anthropologists as authors of articles in successive issues of Ethnohistory. Symbolic of the unequal borrowing by the disciplines is that the single best book, in my opinion, written in the field of American Indian history during the past decade was by anthropologist Edward Spicer, Cycles of Conquest: The Impact of Spain, Mexico, and the United States on the Indians of the Southwest, 1533–1960 (Tucson, 1962).

presumed aboriginal or little changed in the culture and personality of Indian groups by white contact was shown to be deeply influenced by white impact, or at least its aboriginality was questioned.[7] On the other hand, some developments thought the result of white contact may have been aboriginal.[8] At the recent end of the time spectrum, studies of the full range of Indian behavior, from apparently assimilated through professedly native, prompted anthropologists to question the simpler acculturative scales evolved earlier.[9] Even for the time period in between, the studies showed a more complex acculturative and political situation than either anthropologists or historians had appreciated.[10] Likewise, the nascent studies of Pan-Indianism and Indian nationalism moved phenomena once considered peripheral by most historians and anthropologists to a more prominent spot in the arena of Indian history.[11]

Ultimately, anthropologists intended many of their studies to produce one overall theory or set of theories of culture change, whether it involved diffusion, acculturation, or assimilation. Their comparison of social and cultural dynamics indicated recurrence of the same

7 For example, Cara E. Richards, "Huron and Iroquois Residence Patterns, 1600–1650," in Elizabeth Tooker, ed., *Iroquois Culture, History, and Prehistory: Proceedings of the 1965 Conference on Iroquois Research* (Albany, N.Y., 1967), 51–56; Harold Hickerson, "Notes on the Post-Contact Origin of the Midiwin," *Ethnohistory*, IX (1962), 404–423; George L. Hicks, "Cultural Persistence Versus Local Adaptation: Frank G. Speck's Catawba Indians," *ibid.*, XII (1965), 343–354; Deward E. Walker, Jr., "New Light on the Prophet Dance Controversy," *ibid.*, XVI (1969), 245–256.

8 Factions, for example, are now being traced to pre-contact times. E. P. Dozier, "Factionalism at Santa Clara Pueblo," *Ethnology*, V (1966), 172–185.

9 See especially, Malcolm McFee, "The 150% Man, A Product of Blackfeet Acculturation," *American Anthropologist*, LXX (1968), 1096–1107, who also lists some of the previous acculturative scales. Compare the complaint of Harriet J. Kupferer, " 'The Principal People', 1960: A Study of Cultural and Social Groups of The Eastern Cherokee," *Bureau of American Ethnology Bulletin No. 196* (1966) 215–325, especially 311–317.

10 Compare by way of illustration the earlier acculturation studies by Margaret Mead, *The Changing Culture of an Indian Tribe* (New York, 1932), and Felix M. Keesing, "The Menomini Indians of Wisconsin: A Study of Three Centuries of Cultural Contact and Change," *Memoirs of the American Philosophical Society No. 10* (1939), with the recent ones by Theodore Stern, "The Klamath Tribe: A People and Their Reservation," *American Ethnological Society Monograph No. 41* (1965), and Deward E. Walker, Jr., *Conflict and Schism in Nez Perce Acculturation: A Study of Religion and Politics* (Pullman, Wash., 1968).

11 In addition to the article by Robert Thomas cited in note 1, see also Shirley H. Witt, "Nationalistic Trends Among the American Indians," in the same volume, pp. 53–75.

processes of change and resistance but no one all-embracing process. A general trend in the direction of white ways is evident but no certain sequence of change from Indian to white man emerges in each tribe. Failing this end, the studies might have produced a classification of processual possibilities in any given history depending upon such variables in the contact situation as cultural integration, social structure, and relative power of the various parties in interaction. Although some anthropologists claim at times to have achieved such a list, the historian cannot look to these lists for easy adoption of findings but must employ them at best as a checklist of factors to watch for in Indian history.[12]

In conclusion, then, what are the implications of these theoretical and factual developments in recent ethnohistorical and acculturation studies for the writing of a new Indian history? At first glance, details about the Indians' past and present appear clearer at the expense of understanding them or their history. Long considered enigmatic to the white man, the question of what was and is Indian has been made even more perplexing by the anthropologist.[13] Obviously the definition must vary with the tribe and the time studied, but how? If cultural and social persistence and change are basic to a new focus for Indian history, how does one pursue the theme when the dichotomy between aboriginal and white-influenced behavior is obscured as well as

---

[12] An early but important effort is Ralph Linton, ed., *Acculturation in Seven American Indian Tribes* (New York, 1940). The hoped-for ideal is expressed in the statement by the Social Science Research Council Summer Seminar on Acculturation, "Acculturation: An Exploratory Formulation," *American Anthropologist*, LVI (1954), 973–1000. Its culmination is the book edited by Edward H. Spicer, *Perspectives in American Indian Culture Change* (Chicago, 1961). Summaries of books and articles on the subject are compiled in Bernard J. Siegel, ed., "Acculturation: Critical Abstracts, North America," *Stanford Anthropological Series No. 2* (1955).

[13] Viewed in this light, Vine Deloria's strictures upon anthropological obfuscation of the Indians' past and present appear well founded. Viewed in another way, however, it is these very studies of the aboriginal past and the ethnic present said to cause the confusion that meet Deloria's criterion of eliminating abstruseness in favor of individuals' ideas and practices. Many current Indian studies are more complex, hence more confusing, precisely because they emphasize many-sided individuals over the abstract conceptions traditional to anthropology. Thus, no matter how amusing we as historians may find Deloria's remarks upon anthropologists, we can afford to ignore their recent work only at the peril of losing valuable information and perspective upon Indian history. Although Deloria particularly singled out anthropologists for criticism, we must remember that his book, *Custer Died for Your Sins: An Indian Manifesto* (New York, 1969), indicted all would-be white experts upon Indian life for the same fault of abstraction.

clarified by recent studies? If a linear model of acculturation from native Indian to marginal or fully-assimilated white behavior is questioned or denied, how does the historian organize the flow of events in his story? In fact, how does he follow his subject when what is and was Indian are so enigmatic? Considered in this manner, the dilemma of persistence and change leads to confusion about the very unit of study. In short, how were and how are "Indians" to be identified and grouped at various times?[14] Answers to the last question both illustrate the perplexity of the situation and point to one way out of the seeming impasse introduced into Indian history by the dilemma of persistence and change.

As long as anthropologists (or historians) regarded the tribe as the fundamental unit of analysis, then the dynamics of Indian life remained concealed behind abstract conceptions. The traditional theory of the tribe presumed that social, cultural, and territorial boundaries basically coincided. In other words, the social and cultural relationships embraced under the notions of economic, governmental, religious, familial, and other institutional spheres of life were assumed to be contained throughout the body of people designated a tribe. Convenient as such an assumption may have once been for anthropologists in their quest for social integration and cultural configuration, it proves inadequate in coping with the dynamics of social and cultural change. As anthropologists examined change, they increasingly questioned how uniformly and how widely the members of a so-called tribe held one culture and constituted one society. In turning to the processes of diffusion and acculturation, they found social relationships stretching beyond the tribe and the social organization of the groups involved not necessarily coincident with the entire population of the tribe. In line with these findings, the conceptions of culture and society moved from being analytically-given units of analysis to being abstract entities to be synthesized if and when they proved applicable or useful in understanding the actual dynamics of a situation. Likewise, the connections among social organization, culture, and tribe must be determined from empirical data rather than assumed. In fragmenting the unity of tribe, culture, and society, the anthropologists increased the complexity of interpreting Indian life at the same

---

14 One man's view of the perplexities of the problem is given in Frell M. Owl, "Who and What is an Indian," *Ethnohistory*, IX (1962), 265–284.

time as they opened the way to study better the actual individuals and groups involved in the struggle over change and persistence.[15]

Increased attention to the actual agents involved in change and persistence produced a new anthropological awareness of the political dimension in the dynamics of process. Using broader definitions of political behavior as a result of the rise of political anthropology, anthropologists see the nature and degree of persistence and change inextricably entwined with questions of politics and power. If political behavior is broadly defined as competition over public goals involving the struggle for power by groups in the allocation of final authority, then individuals and their allies in promoting or resisting change must engage in some kinds of political activity.[16]

The historian, although not blinded by an elaborate theoretical scheme like the anthropologist, was just as victimized by his implicit assumptions in trying to see beyond the tribe or the reservation to the internal dynamics of Indian life and politics. Even when the historian thought he was portraying the Indian "side" in his writing, he adopted implicitly either the white view of his sources or, equally invidious, the assumption that the outcome of his story was determined more by the white side than by the Indian side. Regardless of the reason, the historian continued to concentrate upon the white "side" of the story even when he professed to be describing the Indian viewpoint. He certainly paid little heed on the whole to the actual Indian-Indian relationships in his story. In brief, the historian treated Indians as passive objects responding to white stimuli rather than as individuals coping creatively in a variety of ways with the different situations in which they found themselves.[17]

Three recent studies of eighteenth-century Cherokee politics and diplomacy illustrate both the current approaches of anthropology and history to Indian scholarship and the implications of these approaches

---

[15] The best introduction to the conceptual difficulties involved in treating the notion of tribe as an analytical unit is June Helm, ed., "Essays on the Problem of Tribe," *Proceedings of the Annual Spring Meeting of the American Ethnological Society* (Seattle and London, 1968).

[16] A similar definition of politics as conceived by political anthropologists is part of the summary of the new field by Arthur Tuden, "Trends in Political Anthropology," *Proceedings of the American Philosophical Society*, CXIII (1969), 336–340.

[17] Elman R. Service directs a similar criticism against Latin American studies in his article, "Indian-European Relations in Colonial Latin America, *American Anthropologist*, LVII (1955), 411–425.

for the writing of a new Indian history. Anthropologist Frederick Gearing employs the story of the efforts of various Cherokee leaders to establish a primitive, tribal-wide state during the period from 1730 to 1780 as an illustration of the new political anthropology. He begins with a lengthy analysis of the alternative social "structural poses" of the Cherokee villages as the inhabitants organized successively for the various tasks of hunting, punishing in-group murder, conducting war and holding general councils, and negotiating peace. Until 1730, according to him, the Cherokee people shared a culture but not an overall political organization. They were divided into independent, politically sovereign villages that formed at the tribal level a "jural community" of peaceful coexistence among Cherokee people. Political decisions and authority were at the village level, not the "tribal" level. For the succeeding decades he describes, first, the efforts of the peace chiefs, or the beloved men, of the various villages to extend their village power structure to the entire jural community. The priest state failed to create a stucture analogous to the village council for the entire people, so the continuing exigencies of war and diplomacy brought the war chiefs to power after 1750 in an attempt to create another tribal-wide governmental organization. The war chiefs' efforts were stymied by the tribal schism caused by the American Revolution, but their power of coercion seemed necessary to the existence of any such state as various Cherokee leaders were said to contemplate.[18]

Historians David Corkran and Henry Malone, using the same kind of sources and dealing with approximately the same period, arrive at quite different conclusions. Corkran devotes an entire monograph to the Cherokee frontier from 1740 to 1762.[19] From the aim espoused in his foreword, he and Gearing should see eye to eye what happened during the period:

This is a book about the Cherokees in the Colonial period—how they behaved and why. It was conceived in the belief that other works dealing with the tribe in this era had not given adequate consideration to Indian motives and objectives. The Cherokees were not only an Indian tribe sustained by a strong cultural tradition; they were a people struggling for nationalism and survival. Their behavior, then, derived from these circumstances. The prob-

---

18 Frederick O. Gearing, "Priests and Warriors: Social Structures for Cherokee Politics in the 18th Century," *American Anthropological Association Memoir No. 93* (1962)

19 David H. Corkran, *The Cherokee Frontier: Conflict and Survival, 1740–62* (Norman, 1962).

lem of the historian is to understand their culture, their intra-tribal problems, and their international situation. It is not sufficient to approach their
story from the point of view of the advancing and victorious white. The
records available for the period are, of course, those of the Colonials. From
them I have attempted to sift the purely Indian material and to permit it
to speak for itself.[20]

According to his narrative, however, Cherokee efforts at tribal-wide
government were due as much or more to Carolinian, Virginian, and
French use of the various chiefs as pawns in white diplomacy as to
Cherokee cultural tradition. He depicts Cherokee leaders and villages
divided by factions according to whom they supported among the conflicting whites and which whites supported them. Essentially, Corkran
focuses more on the nexus of white-Indian diplomatic relationships
than on the Indian-Indian political activity. Another historian, Henry T. Malone, asserts baldly what Corkran implies. Surveying the
eighteenth-century political organization as prelude to the developments of the first three decades of the next century, Malone bluntly
states that the "pseudo-national Cherokee governments" developed
solely at the behest of the whites and amounted to nothing in the face
of traditional local village autonomy.[21]

Although the three studies are not necessarily irreconcilable in their
findings, they do represent quite opposite ways of viewing Indian history and interpreting sources. All three men used ethnographic reconstructions of aboriginal Cherokee culture and historical documents
on the developments they studied. Both Gearing and Corkran used
the same kind of sources, but Corkran found far more. Perhaps, then,
the difference between his and Gearing's conclusions result from
Corkran's better information. On the other hand, although Corkran
mentions far more Indian names and possesses more information than
Gearing, his perspective is on white-Indian relations. Gearing is not
unaware of white diplomacy and even makes that the primary cause
for the attempts at tribal-wide government, but he focuses upon
Indian-Indian relations and relegates white men to the background of
his analysis. Gearing delineates divisions among the chiefs according
to their views upon the nature and need for a new state; Corkran por-
trays them divided according to white power and alliance. Corkran

---

20 *Ibid.*, vii.
21 Henry T. Malone, *Cherokees of the Old South: A People in Transition* (Athens, Ga.,
1956), 24–27.

pictures the Cherokee governmental structure as relatively fixed during the same time that Gearing stresses great change. Corkran either denies or fails to see the difference between war and peace chiefs and the effects of a matrilineal kinship system, while Gearing presumes these facts essential to his entire analysis. Malone agrees with Gearing on the importance of these aspects of Cherokee culture but maintains that only the traditional local system of politics operated in the situation. Puzzling as the three men leave the field of eighteenth-century Cherokee history, the lessons to be learned from their differences appear amply clear.

First, interpretation and evaluation of sources are inextricably and mutually related. In order to evaluate the reliability of the data, whether white or Indian produced, the historian needs to know the political processes that produced the data in the first place. Conversely, the historian must use those sources produced by the political process to reconstruct the political forms and behavior of the people. If, as in the case of the Cherokee, the forms of government were in flux or evolving into new forms, then the analyst's task becomes even harder in evaluating the reliability of the data and interpreting its implications for government and politics. Furthermore, a dramatic change in political process could result as easily from efforts to preserve the native past from other tribes' or white influences as from attempts to introduce new patterns of society or culture.

Second, the interpretations of sources and overall perspective are also mutually related. As these three studies demonstrate, historians and anthropologists change some of their outward practices—just as they say the Indians they study do—only better to retain their long customary, basic viewpoints. Despite the tokenism of ethnohistory, the gap in perspective between history and anthropology seems as wide as ever in these works on the Cherokee. In this case, the fundamental perspectives of the two disciplines determined whether white or Indian behavior was made the dependent or independent variable, so-to-speak. The historians chose the white actions as the cause of the Indian actions, while Gearing portrayed Indian activities as self-originated and creative responses to white-posed problems. Although we cannot choose between the validity of the conclusions of the three men in the present state of research because of the different perspectives they used in interpreting their sources, it is obvious that it takes far more to accomplish Corkran's goal as espoused in his foreword than

the simple professing of it. Perspective is a matter of theory and outlook as well as moral judgment, and writing a new Indian history will
take more than good will in combination with old approaches.[22] Important as knowledge of the external political environment of Indian
peoples may be to understanding their political behavior, it is no substitute for understanding the internal processes. Rather than treating
tribal political behavior as some sort of static given, historians must
demonstrate carefully just what is the nature of political organization
in a so-called tribe and the role it plays in Indian-Indian and Indian-
white relations. To read sources as if all Indian names were uncon-
nected to a political context within a tribe, in addition to any nexus
with whites or other Indian peoples, is to substitute stereotype for the
actual dynamics of Indian life.

Third, to translate the problems of persistence and change into a
political context presumes a knowledge of Indian political processes
and forms that is difficult to obtain given the newness of political anthropology as a field. Valuable as the new political interest and the
comparative view of this latest offspring of anthropology promises to
be eventually in terms of theory and data, the field in its present state
offers conceptual awareness more than validated findings, as Gearing's
study illustrates. His work was presented as an exercise in political
anthropology as much as an examination of Cherokee politics. He
may be correct in his analysis of Cherokee politics but only further research will tell. As his study does show, political anthropology provides awareness in the form of definitions and checklists of possible
governmental forms as a result of its comparative perspective rather
than full-fledged results easily adoptable by the historian. In these circumstances, the historian can use the new field for its perspective but
must suspect its findings. Thus, he should scrutinize the evidence and
the conclusions of the political anthropologist with the same suspicion
he would any other source of information. Although inappropriate to
summarize the field here, it may be worthwhile to discuss briefly the

---

22 Lest I seem too harsh in my criticism of Corkran, let me call attention to his second
and broader study, *The Creek Frontier, 1540–1783* (Norman, 1957). I have also attributed
an Indian political organization to white auspices in my article, "Barrier to Settlement:
British Indian Policy in the Old Northwest, 1783–1794," in David M. Ellis, ed., *The
Frontier in American Development: Essays in Honor of Paul W. Gates* (Ithaca, N.Y.,
1969), 249–276.

definitions and conceptual approach of the field in order to suggest its significance for studying the political context of sources and the synthesis of facts in Indian history.[23]

With the new emphasis upon process rather than formal structure, anthropologists of Indian political life are going beyond the older presentation of patterns of kinship as the only, or at least primary, description of political organization and process in all Indian societies —all of which proved so uninformative to historians for their understanding of power and politics in a tribe during a specific historic period. With perspective broadened by attention to African, Asian, and other non-Western societies, anthropologists have widened political science definitions of political activities and forms to embrace any process of public competition to influence outcomes for the group as a whole. The greater appreciation of the political aspects in the making and executing of all public decisions, the maintenance of public support and an air of legitimacy during these times, and the use of persuasion and influence as well as force in political activity places the anthropologists' new interest in line with a traditional concern of historians, and perhaps offers a new ground for the revival of ethnohistory as a joint endeavor of historians and anthropologists.

As a result of the broader definition of political behavior, the arena of politics encompasses conflict and its resolution in whatever area of society it may be found, whether called religious, economic, political, or otherwise. The size of the arena and the groups involved may be as large, greater, or smaller than the social relationships embodied in what is usually designated as the tribe among North American Indians. When considered in the full context of the political process, the political system, and the overall political environment, the tribe often appears to be an artificial unit of analysis. To presume a priori, therefore, that the tribe is always the relevant unit of the political system draws attention from the individual people and the specific behavior in intra-tribal politics as much as it does in inter-tribal and white-Indian relations.

In fact, the tribe becomes but one kind of socio-political unit in the

---

23 The newness of the field and its conceptual approach may be traced in the two articles by David Easton and Edwin Winckler on "Political Anthropology," in Bernard J. Siegel, ed., *Biennial Review of Anthropology* (Stanford, 1959, 1970), 210–262, and 301–386, respectively.

descriptive taxonomy of the new field. Comparison of African, Asian, American, and other so-called tribes reveals the spectrum of possibilities and sharpens the definition of the entity but not with universal agreement upon its attributes. What is agreed upon is that none of the so-called tribes living in the area of the continental United States aboriginally possessed a governmental structure designated a state, if a state is defined minimally as a full-time, centralized, institutionalized administrative structure with a monopoly of the coercive power in the society. Perhaps a few peoples on the southeastern coast of what is now the United States approached this end of the political spectrum. On the other end of the spectrum was the band which was found primarily among the peoples of the Great Basin and southern California. Bands refer to systems comprised of small groups of families living apart and with no specialization beyond age and sex-graded activities. In theory, there is little or no separation of political authority from lines of descent and kinship relations. The processes of decision-making, opinion-formation, and adjudication and execution extend at most beyond the family to the small group of the band, never to the entire people later called the tribe by whites. The majority of aboriginal Indian societies in the United States ranged between the ends of the spectrum in the realm called tribes and chiefdoms.[24]

From the definitions of the two ends of the spectrum, it is clear that the criteria for classifying the various political systems revolve about the connection between (1) the nature and dispersion of power among a people and (2) the degree of formalization, centralization, and specialization of the governmental structure. According to these criteria and regardless of whether groups are called bands, tribes, chiefdoms, or confederacies, political decision-making and authority among Indian peoples in the United States before white contact resided in units territorially smaller than those later designated tribal. Even in the fabled League of the Iroquois, political power rested almost entirely in the

---

[24] Introductions to the characteristics of the various governments and their social attributes are provided in the "Foundations of Modern Anthropology Series"; see, for example, Elman R. Service, *The Hunters* (Englewood Cliffs, N. J., 1966); Marshall R. Sahlins, *Tribesmen* (Englewood Cliffs, N. J., 1968); Lawrence R. Krader, *Formation of the State* (Englewood Cliffs, N. J., 1968). Compare Winckler, "Political Anthropology," pp. 306–329, for the use and criticism of this taxonomy. A brief survey of North American Indian governments is provided by Harold E. Driver, *Indians of North America* (Chicago, 1961), 325–352. See also W. H. Sears, "The State in Certain Areas and Periods of the Prehistoric Southeastern United States," *Ethnohistory*, IX (1962), 109–125.

hands of local chiefs in local communities.[25] Some Plains Indians' political associations embraced units beyond kindred and local community to reach a tribal-wide extent, but they were transitory, situational devices, not full-time government.[26] All so-called tribes in the United States had governmental institutions of some kind, but none outside the Southeast had a full-time, centralized, power-wielding government embracing the entire tribal territory. Tribes may have been jural communities, to use Gearing's term, but not sovereign entities as such, for polity and society were not coexistensive aboriginally.[27]

As the previous discussion implies, the tribe as a political entity in the area of the United States is in nearly all instances a post-white contact development. Certainly, tribal-wide, centralized systems of government arose in most cases only after, and often in response to, white contact. Thus the chronicle of the Cherokee state begun by Gearing and Corkran reaches fulfillment only in the 1820s with the creation of a republic and the adoption of a written constitution. The constitution provided for a centralized government patterned after the by-then familiar white model with a chief, a vice-chief, two-house legislature, and supreme court.[28] Like the Cherokees, other tribes under the pressure of white intrusions, the demands for land cessions, and the urging of missionaries and government agents developed tribal-wide governments.[29] Even these forces, as the Navajo example demonstrates, proved insufficient for generations to overcome old habits of local autonomy in some tribes. Not until the efforts of the federal government

---

25 The best introduction to this complex topic is William N. Fenton, "Locality as a Basic Factor in the Development of Iroquois Social Structure," in Fenton, ed., "Symposium on Local Diversity in Iroquois Culture," *Bureau of American Ethnology Bulletin No.* 149 (1951), 35–54.

26 Lawrence Krader, *Formation of the State*, 30, 33–35, points out this vital distinction.

27 As a result of the broader framework introduced by political anthropology, we might at long last move beyond the dispute about the nature of the tribe and particularly its territoriality engendered by the Indian Claims Cases. Some important theoretical articles resulting from anthropologists fighting these cases are Alfred L. Kroeber, "Nature of the Land-Holding Group," *Ethnohistory*, II (1955), 303–314; Robert A. Manners, "Tribe and Tribal Boundaries: The Walapai," *ibid.*, IV (1957), 1–26; Anthony F. C. Wallace, "Political Organization and Land Tenure Among the Northeastern Indians, 1600-1830," *Southwestern Journal of Anthropology*, XIII (1957), 301–321.

28 Malone, *Cherokees of the Old South*, 74–90, gives a brief summary of this development. Even after the establishment of this government, it is still unclear from my research whether the system was more coercive than previous local authority.

29 Lester Hargrett offers an annotated list of some of the documents produced by these governments during the nineteenth century in *A Bibliography of the Constitutions and Laws of the American Indians* (Cambridge, 1947).

under the Indian Reorganization Act in the 1930s was there even a token tribal-wide government among the Navajo, and the effective, well-organized tribal council of today is a post-World War II invention.[30] The ethnic identity of many a tribe as a jural community may have been post-white contact also. It is uncertain after reading the leading authorities on the Delawares, for example, whether the various "Delawaran" communities with their different dialects and extreme autonomy considered themselves to be one people before the historic period.[31]

The value of this governmental taxonomy to the historian lies in its calling attention to the possibilities of changing political form rather than in providing a sure guide to that change. The historian cannot assume that Indian peoples moved in certain sequence from band to tribe to chiefdom to state as Peter Farb implied in the title of his book, *Man's Rise to Civilization as Shown by the Indians of North America from Primeval Times to the Coming of the Industrial State.*[32] The taxonomy proves not to be an evolutionary sequence of stages in history when compared against evidence of actual development. It can and should be used as a typological device to provide a checklist of alternatives in exploring the actual development in a given case. The analyst can employ the taxonomy against the ethnocentric political biases of the white creators of so many sources in Indian history to find the real political machinery behind those "chiefs" and "kings" so visible to the whites of the time. Needless to say, the concentration upon Indian political process in its own terms will encourage the historian to make greater use of Indian government records themselves.[33] Regardless of its use, the taxonomy only points to possibilities, for the analyst must always remember that the forms might be changing and that the confusion of the sources reflects this fact. Whites of the past created the confusion of the tribe by their ethnocentric translation of Indian political behavior according to white conceptions of the

---

30 Mary Shepardson, "Navajo Ways in Government: A Study in Political Process," *American Anthropological Association Memoir No. 96* (1963).

31 Compare William W. Newcomb, Jr., "The Culture and Acculturation of the Delaware Indians," *University of Michigan Anthropological Paper No. 10* (1956), 84–86, with the review of this monograph by Anthony Wallace in *Ethnohistory*, IV (1957), 322–323.

32 New York, 1968.

33 John A. Noon provides an example of the use of such records in "Law and Government of the Grand River Iroquois," *Viking Fund Publications in Anthropology No. 12* (New York, 1949). Anna G. Kilpatrick and Jack F. Kilpatrick edited some of these documents in "Chronicles of Wolftown: Social Documents of the North Carolina Cherokees, 1850–1862," *Bureau of American Ethnology Bulletin No. 196* (1966), 1–111.

nation-state and supreme sovereignty. Anthropologists compounded the original confusion by merging political into social and cultural organization. The taxonomy removes these blinders but should not be allowed to impose its own through analysts who may assume that it can do more than present an awareness of possibilities.

Complicating the application of the governmental taxonomy to Indian history is the prevalence of factions among the tribes. In spite of its widespread presence in Indian life past and present, the study of the phenomena that goes under the name of factionalism is little advanced beyond the superficial description given by Ralph Linton in 1936:

Among American Indians the pattern of factions is certainly deep-seated. In some cases two factions have survived for generations, changing leaders and the bases of their disputes and winning some individuals from each other, but remaining distinct social entities in constant opposition to each other. This opposition seems to be their main reason for existence, their policy and declared grounds for opposition shifting with the circumstances. In many cases any cause which is espoused by one will immediately be resisted by the other.[34]

Analysts since then have tried, with few agreed-upon results, to describe and classify the nature of the conflict, the structure of the divisions, and the conditions generating factions. Generally these classificatory schemes concern whether means or ends are in dispute, the number of areas of life involved (economic, religious, political, and so forth), whether groupings are transient or permanent, what is the internal organization and how institutionalized, and whether factional cleavage is aboriginal or post-contact. In fact, at the present stage of knowledge no one even knows whether all the divisions described as factions are a single analytical category.[35]

To some extent these problems of theory result from the lack of

---

34 Ralph Linton, *The Study of Man* (New York, 1936), 229.

35 In addition to the works cited in the succeeding two notes, the reader interested in general treatments of factionalism should consult William N. Fenton, "Factionalism in American Indian Society," *Proceedings of the Fourth International Congress of Anthropology and Ethnology* (Vienna, 1952), II, 330–340; Alan R. Beals and Bernard J. Siegel, *Divisiveness and Social Conflict: An Anthropological Approach* (Stanford, 1966); J. S. Yadava, "Factionalism in a Haryana Village," *American Anthropologist*, LXX (1968), 898–910; Spicer, *Cycles of Conquest*, 492–501; Ralph W. Nicholas, "Factions: A Comparative Analysis," in *Political Systems and the Distribution of Power* (Association of Social Anthropologists Monograph No. 2; London, 1965), 21–61.

facts about factionalism, for historians and anthropologists generally neglect it or relegate it to the periphery of their studies. Although no student of Indian societies doubts the ubiquity nor the importance of factions in Indian affairs past or present, little attention has been paid to chronicling the history of these internal divisions.[36] Even for those peoples like the Cherokees or the Iroquois, where factional divisions may be traced for at least two centuries, or for the Nez Perce and some Pueblos, where factions have been found for over a century, we still do not possess specific lists of personnel and issues over time. Only after we gather this sort of information can we determine such basic questions as how continuous were the members and their families and the issues throughout the history of the factional politics, let alone generalize about the causes, composition, and effects of factionalism.[37] Determining, for example, whether factions were genetic in membership and continuity would go far in indicating the nature of conditions necessary for their persistence and their effects. In other words, analysis cannot proceed very far unless we first obtain a much more detailed description of the phenomenon or phenomena of factionalism.

Although much is thus unknown about factionalism in fact and in theory, it figures so prominently in past and present Indian life that the historian, regardless of ignorance, must reckon with its effects for both the interpretation and evaluation of sources. As with other areas of political anthropology, the chief value of current studies of factionalism is to provide an awareness of the possible political context of sources. Whether considering persistence or change in government or other aspects of an Indian society or culture, the historian must always

---

36 On their ubiquity today, see the opinion of James A. Clifton, "Factional Conflict and the Indian Community: The Prairie Potawatomie Case," in Levine and Lurie, eds., *The American Indian Today,* 115. For the past, see Linton, ed., *Acculturation in Seven American Indian Tribes,* passim, and Spicer, ed., *Perspectives in American Indian Culture Change,* passim.

37 Suggestive of the possibilities on Iroquois factionalism are Robert F. Berkhofer, Jr., "Faith and Factionalism Among the Senecas; Theory and Ethnohistory," *Ethnohistory,* XII (1965), 99–112; Thomas S. Abler, "Seneca Nation Factionalism: The First Twenty Years," in Tooker, ed., *Iroquois Culture, History, and Prehistory,* 25–26; Alex F. Ricciardelli, "Factionalism at Oneida, An Iroquois Indian Community" (Ph.D. dissertation, University of Michigan, 1961). Glimpses of Cherokee factionalism may be seen in the standard political histories: Malone, *Cherokees of the Old South;* Marion L. Starkey, *The Cherokee Nation* (New York, 1946); Morris L. Wardell, *A Political History of the Cherokee Nation, 1838–1907* (Norman, 1938). A century of Nez Perce factionalism is the subject of Walker, *Conflict and Schism in Nez Perce Acculturation.* On factionalism in the pueblos, see, among others, David H. French, "Factionalism in Isleta Pueblo," *American Ethnological Society Monograph No. 14* (1948); David M. Brugge, "Pueblo Factionalism and External Relations," *Ethnohistory,* XVI (1969), 191–200.

watch the factional provenience of his sources. Many historical documents are the product of one side of a factional split, though they may purport to represent or are interpreted to apply to the whole tribe. Thus, all members of the tribe are described as thinking or doing what only one part thought or did. Such one-sidedness can effect the answers to a whole series of questions important to Indian history: Who were the chiefs and what was the nature of government in a tribe at a certain time? What was the nature of the support for certain leaders in proposed innovations, treaties, or other actions? How acculturated were the various members of the tribe at various times? Whether factions even existed or not might have different answers from different sides. Examples of these questions are not hard to find. Supposedly, the validity of the treaty of 1838 with the Senecas depended legally upon the number of chiefs in the tribe, but this very point had been in contention among the Seneca factions for at least five years prior to the treaty.[38] Again, the Cherokee treaties of the 1830s and the whole issue of support for removal are beclouded by factional dispute reflected in the documents.[39] As these examples illustrate even in their brevity, sources are frequently the product of factional dispute and to read only one side conceals the record and denies the historic situation producing the contradictory evidence. Discerning the factional provenience of documents and other sources is as important for understanding the dynamics of Indian-Indian as for Indian-white relations.

This warning applies also to anthropological sources, whether theory or data, fieldnotes or published monograph. To what extent is the nature and persistence of the aboriginal patterns found by the anthropologist a function of his informant's factional affiliation? Some of the amazing continuity that anthropologist William Fenton finds in Iroquois custom between his fieldwork and that of Lewis Henry Morgan may result from their reliance on the same Seneca faction and even family as informants.[40] Certainly any anthropologist's fieldnotes and

---

[38] My unpublished manuscript on Seneca factionalism, 1790–1860, presents this story in detail.

[39] See the books on this tribe cited in note 37, but the full range of political behavior remains to be told from the sources.

[40] The Parker family as anthropological informants can be traced in William Fenton's introductions to Lewis H. Morgan, *League of the Ho-Dé-No-Sau-Nee, Iroquois* (Corinth ed., New York, 1962); and *Parker on The Iroquois* (Syracuse, 1968); and his article, "Tonawanda Longhouse Ceremonies: Ninety Years After Lewis Henry Morgan," *Bureau of American Ethnology Bulletin No. 128* (1941), 140–166.

articles, valuable as they may be, must be checked for factional bias. So, too, with acculturative studies. Are the various categories of the "Indian" to "white" continuum a reflection of previous factional history? Certainly, that was the case in the past in certain tribes.[41] Is the phenomenon of persistence the result or the reflection of factional **cleavage in a tribe? In short, who and what is and was "Indian"** seems closely tied to factional disputes past and present in many tribes. Thus, succeeding studies of acculturation may not be refinements of data and concept so much as a reflection of the changing characteristics of tribal life and political factionalism. If modern anthropologists have always worked under these conditions, then their findings on aboriginal and contemporary culture and society should reflect the stage of factionalism and acculturation in a tribe when they entered. Their productions can be used, therefore, as history in a way they perhaps had not intended. On the other hand, their work may represent only one side of the tale, so-to-speak. Once again the motto of the historian must be: Beware of the anthropologist bearing conclusions.[42]

The effects of factionalism can be viewed according to a variety of perspectives. According to one perspective, the results may be measured by their function in tribal integration. Seen in one way, factionalism disrupts tribal solidarity and hinders collective action, but seen in another it perhaps drains internal hostilities generated within an Indian society from more aggressive intramural behavior. In the latter view, factionalism provides a flexibility within those Indian societies that had few or no other means for resolving internal conflict. According to another perspective, factionalism can be looked at in terms of how it preserves or changes Indian ways of life. Nancy Lurie hypothesizes that such internal divisions promoted social and cultural survival because their presence meant "no outsider could gain total dominance for his programs aimed in one way or another at reducing Indian distinctiveness."[43] Other theorists argue that factions hastened acculturation by internalizing the promotion of the proposed changes

---

41 For example, Walker, *Conflict and Schism in Nez Perce Acculturation;* Robert F. Berkhofer, Jr., *Salvation and the Savage: An Analysis of Protestant Missions and American Indian Response, 1787–1862* (Lexington, Ky., 1965), 125–151. Perhaps what Kupferer wants to treat as a refinement of the acculturative scale in her "The Principle People" really reflects the changing nature of the tribe.

42 This motto would seem equally applicable to use of the new Indian oral archives material.

43 In "Historical Background," Levine and Lurie, eds., *The American Indian Today,* 38.

by one side. For example, as one side tried to urge or force its program upon fellow tribesmen, it obliged the other side to cope with change.[44] The validity of all these contradictory perspectives depends as much upon theoretical frameworks as upon evidence.

So once again we come full circle to a recurring theme in this article: interpretation of sources, the writing of Indian history, and perspective are all mutually related. As in studying other aspects of Indian politics, the historian must use the awareness of factions to evaluate and interpret his sources. At the same time, he utilizes the same set of sources to determine the nature, extent, and effects of factionalism. The perspective and the theoretical framework enable the analyst to read evidence and derive facts, but those facts in turn are synthesized according to the perspective and theory of the analyst. Only by combining interpretation, perspective, and theory can the historian reveal the complexity of Indian politics and life.

Toward this end let me suggest in general some possible connections between factionalism and Indian political systems. Factionalism could both facilitate and delay change in the form of tribal government. At times the very presence of factions forced the community or society to seek a new form of social integration in the form of a new, more elaborately organized government. The existence of factions indicated the desirability of substituting a new set of political relations for the old, if the group wanted internal peace. In short, factionalism could only be resolved by two sides forming a new kind of government or by one side leaving the political arena through exile or the elimination of influence. If the former alternative was chosen, then factionalism probably promoted transformation of government only to thwart its operation in the end. The failure of factions to become true political parties with a belief in the legitimacy of opposition frustrated the successful operation of the new government. One faction would challenge the legitimacy and authority of the government established by the other. At the same time as dual political parties failed to develop, factionalism continued and so may be said to be an institutionalized phenomenon but without explicit tribal approval. For this reason and others, factionalism expanded the political arena beyond the local community to the entire tribe or society in the quest for authoritative power. Thus, factionalism was responsible in many cases for making

---

44 Walker, *Conflict and Schism in Nez Perce Acculturation*, 133–139.

the transition from community to tribal-wide government so that jural and sovereign communities coincided.[45] Regardless of the speed or certainty of such a sequence of developments in a tribe, these political possibilities help explain the problem of who was a chief. In every case, traditional leadership was in question, and the criteria for selection had broadened but without any society-wide agreement.

As tribal political arenas organized, elites may have formed in some of the larger tribes. For example, among the Cherokee and Choctaw tribes in the west during the 1850s, the factional struggle told in the documents seems to reflect cleavage within a top set of governmental leaders more than between the basic language and cultural divisions of the tribes. In some ways, these two tribes resembled Robert Redfield's conception of a peasant society, for there occurred "a relatively stable and very roughly typical adjustment between local and national life, a developed larger social system in which there are two cultures of upper and lower halves."[46] Intermediate between the national American culture and the modified native culture was the elite which possessed its own distinct way of life. Further comparative work must be done before such tribes as the Cherokee and Choctaw of the mid-nineteenth century can be safely characterized as peasant, but the possibility of factionalism assuming this form of development must be taken into account in interpreting political conflict from the documents of these and other Indian peoples in the United States.[47]

Surely the kind of factionalism we have been examining concerns the element of power in relation to questions of change and persistence among a people. Whether pre- or post-white contact, whether aboriginal or acculturative, the groups in dispute contest for overall public acceptance of their view of the issue. Factions arise and persist in these circumstances because of the situation of powerlessness present in so many tribes. Factions rather than parties develop when leaders and their followers cannot enforce their decisions for an entire

---

45 Among others, see Gearing, *Priests and Warriors;* Berkhofer, *Salvation and the Savage,* 125–151; Walker, *Conflict and Schism in Nez Perce Acculturation.*

46 Robert Redfield, *Peasant Society and Culture: An Anthropological Approach to Civilization* (Chicago, 1956), 65, but see all of chap. 2.

47 That the Cherokee and Choctaw tribes met the criteria for being peasant societies first occurred to me when reading the reports of the missionaries in the papers of the American Board of Commissioners for Foreign Missions deposited at Houghton Library, Harvard University. In addition to Redfield, see also Eric R. Wolf, *Peasants* (Englewood Cliffs, N. J., 1966).

society, and Indian history is the story of powerlessness in at least two senses. Under the colonial conditions imposed by United States reservation policy, even if Indians organized tribal-wide government they lacked the ultimate authority without federal sanction to execute their will against the opposition. Complicating their situation is the aboriginal belief in consensus. What Edward Spicer claims was the connection between authority and consent in all societies of the Southwest obtained in most tribes in what is now the United States:

It seems very doubtful that what modern men know as "difference of opinion" existed for more than very short periods of time in any of the communities of the Indians in northwestern New Spain before the coming of white men. This is not to say that new ideas never appeared with reference to community government, religious ceremonies, and other aspects of living. They of course did appear as gradual growths, resulting from the constant discussion of community affairs by successive generations of older men and women and by slow shifts of opinion from adherence to one strong man's viewpoint to that of another. In other words, there is no reason to believe that these societies any more than others in the world were wholly static. But it does not appear that any of the Indians expected as a constant feature of community life any basic differences of viewpoint. Their plans of government were posited upon another foundation which in brief may be summarized as the principle of unanimity. . . . In [their] meetings it was sometimes expected that the men would not have the same views at the beginning, especially in some matter that was felt to be a crisis. . . . It was, however, the expectation that by the time the matter had been thoroughly discussed, all would be of the same view, so that statements were always turned eventually into consensus in terms in which the group felt and acted and in terms of which it became organized to face the crisis. In other words, the general meetings were posited on the feeling that unity could always be achieved and that difference of view would not persist after thorough discussion.[48]

Such was the ideal in most tribes and violations of it could rarely be punished given the ideal and the lack of power of Indian governments. Thus cultural ideals, tribal political organization, and federal Indian policy all contributed to make factionalism a common form of Indian politics. Given these conditions, factionalism was a creative response to external white pressures as well as to internal cultural values, and

---

[48] Spicer, *Cycles of Conquest*, 492. Some of the implications of this attitude for power and authority in a tribe are drawn in Walter B. Miller, "Two Concepts of Authority," *American Anthropologist*, LVII (1955), 271–289; and Bruce G. Trigger, "Order and Freedom in Huron Society," *Anthropologica*, n.s., V (1963), 151–169.

its chronicling provides an Indian view of an Indian way of handling change and persistence.

Factions may prove as significant in the formation of inter-tribal political relationships as in intra-tribal ones. If the notion of the tribe is mainly a white stereotype, then that of the Indian is wholly so. If the development of the tribe as a socio-political unit must be built up from its local communities, then regional and national all-Indian organizations must be traced in the same way. As with the creation of tribal-wide political organization, so the formation of inter-tribal organizations may have been in response to white contact but the true all-Indian ones must be considered a creative solution to the problems facing tribes. The politics of the formation of most confederacies is not well known, and the story of national Indian organizations is not well told. It may have been contacts made at boarding schools, white-called conferences, and other white-stimulated beginnings that form the background of recent regional and national organizations, but the peyote religion, regional powwows, and the National Congress of American Indians or the younger National Indian Youth Council are inter-tribal organizational solutions in Indian terms. As such the role of factions is indicated but not well chronicled.[49]

These hypotheses about intra- and inter-tribal political organization point to the problem of, and one possible basis for, an overall history of the Indians in the United States. Tribal histories offer grave problems of perspective and organization but the writing of a general history adds difficulties nearly impossible to overcome in conception and theory as well. Somehow the diversity of many cultures and societies, the various times of migration and contact, and the different sequences of diffusion and acculturative processes of the many tribes must be combined with the uniformity of certain overall trends. The similarity of the processes exemplified in all tribes must not conceal a variety of outcomes and histories; nor must the multiplicity of details in different time settings be allowed to hide common trends and repetitive processes. Ideally, a general history of Indians in the United States should fuse the general and recurring in Indian history with the uniqueness of the stories of specific individuals and the concrete

---

49 Some hints are provided in J. S. Slotkin, *The Peyote Religion: A Study in Indian-White Relations* (Glencoe, Ill., 1956), *passim*; Thomas, "Pan-Indianism," 82, Newcomb, *Culture and Acculturation of the Delaware Indians*, 118–122.

social and cultural entities in the multitude of tribes. He who would essay a general history must organize it according to general unifying themes and yet preserve the diversity and complexity of the individual histories.[50] Sequences, cycles, or something comparable can provide the basis of organization, but they cannot be allowed to obscure the richness of individual lives or tribal stories. In my opinion, focus upon the politics and changing governmental systems offers one way of achieving these ends. Tracing the complex history of persistence and change through its political context from jural communities within the tribe to a tribal-wide political arena, from confederacies and regional cooperation to the national organizations of today exposes individual Indians to view as they favored or opposed actions in coping with situations confronting their societies. It presents the possibilities they saw in various situations and the means they used for the resultant outcomes in the general overall story of transition from American Indians to Indian Americans. Yet the political view of Indian history, while crucial to its interpretation, is only one way of looking at persistence and change in the story of American Indians. Other aspects of culture, society, and personality all belong to the complete story of the Indians in the United States. All I mean to argue here is that politics provides a critical if not central focus for interpreting change and persistence in other areas of Indian life over time.

The political context also affords some glimpse of Indian history from the Indian point of view. No historian, let alone one of Indian life be he red or white, ever completely captures the multiplicity of views upon events held by past peoples as they lived them. Formal history cannot be folk history, although the folk view can be useful to the historian.[51] At best he can offer some glimpse of these views in combination with perspectives unseen and unknown to the actors of the time because of his knowledge of the future they knew not. In many ways the political context allows such a merger of views because it concentrates upon Indians as individuals coping with the world as they see it through their leaders. Stress upon the dynamics of the

---

50 A theoretical statement of the problem of synthesis is Philip Dark, "Methods of Synthesis in Ethnohistory," *Ethnohistory*, IV (1957), 231–278.

51 The distinction between the two kinds of history is the topic of Charles Hudson, "Folk History and Ethnohistory," *Ethnohistory*, XIII (1966), 52–70. The general problem of relating actors' and observers' views of history is the basic theme of my *A Behavioral Approach to Historical Analysis* (New York and London, 1969).

changing situation introduces the dimension of time into the study. Moreover, examination of the whole range of political behavior includes a fuller spectrum of Indian opinion and action than heretofore available. It makes individuals, if not heroes, of more Indians than before because it includes men who pursued the politics of the possible as well as those who failed in noble causes. Religious leaders and war chiefs, politicians and statesmen all receive their due place in the story according to their role in the broadly defined political arena. Such a democratic view of the participants in Indian history opens a wider rather than narrower moral perspective upon the subject. Heroes are not defined by a single moral criterion but by their role in the political process of their time.[52] Furthermore, the simple decline and death theme so prevalent in the writing of Indian history can be transformed into a more complex moral judgment by noting multiple declines and renascences. As suggested by Anthony Wallace's long title, *The Death and Rebirth of the Seneca: The History and Culture of the Great Iroquois Nation, Their Destruction and Demoralization, and Their Cultural Revival at the Hands of the Indian Visionary, Handsome Lake,*[53] the history of a tribe can be seen as a series of renascences according to varying forms of activity which revitalize and reorient Indian life. In fact, the Indian of today can be seen just as easily as having added much to *his* way of life by grafting what he wants of white culture to his own values and attitudes. He becomes a 150% man in one anthropologist's terms.[54] Certainly such views will provide a complex heritage to meet the political demands for a new Indian history. Red experience like that of all peoples is complex and its history ought be no less so. The political perspective offers one way of reconstructing, interpreting, and organizing the past of Indians to suggest that complexity.

---

[52] For example, Alvin M. Josephy allows only one kind of "patriotism" in tribal politics in his *The Patriot Chiefs: A Chronicle of American Indian Leadership* (New York, 1961).

[53] New York, 1970.

[54] McFee, "The 150% Man," cited in note 9 above.

The Indian and the Civilian Conservation Corps

DONALD L. PARMAN

Donald Parman is a member of the history department in Purdue University.

A RECENT STUDY of the Negro in the Civilian Conservation Corps gives an appalling picture of racial prejudice and discrimination in a program which is usually considered as the most enlightened and progressive of the New Deal. The author shows that Negroes had suffered terribly from the depression before 1933 because of job displacement and lack of welfare facilities. Even after the advent of the New Deal, southern administrators refused to select a fair share of Negroes for the CCC, and the black enrollees, when admitted, faced constant hostility and segregation both within the organization and from whites near the camps. Robert Fechner, director of CCC, consistently accepted such conditions and refused to support Washington subordinates who sought to remove at least some of the discrimination against Negroes.[1] Did Indians in CCC, like the Negroes, demonstrate an acute need for the economic and rehabilitative benefits of CCC only to receive a token share in the program?

In terms of depression privations, the Indian's condition often paralleled or exceeded that of the Negro. Indians, with few exceptions, lived in chronic poverty even during the prosperous 1920s. The Meriam Commission reported in its voluminous independent study of 1928 that 46.8 percent of American Indians lived on a per capita income of $100 to $200 per year, while only 2.2 percent received incomes over $500 per year.[2] The Indians' situation became worse when

---

[1] John A. Salmond, "The Civilian Conservation Corps and the Negro," *Journal of American History*, LII (1965), 75–88.

[2] Lewis Meriam, et al., *The Problem of Indian Administration* (Baltimore, 1928), 447. The Meriam Commission consisted of ten experts in various fields that made an independent study of Indian affairs in 1926 and 1927. The Institute for Government Research conducted the study with a grant from the Rockefeller family. The members of the commission visited Indian reservations, schools, hospitals, and other facilities for seven months before writing a voluminous report covering such matters as health, economic

the depression curtailed or terminated their normal revenues from land leases, sale of oil and timber, wage work, and handicrafts. By late 1933, after the start of federal relief programs, Indians' per capita income stood at only $81 per year.[3]

Treatment of the Indian in CCC, however, took a much different course than that accorded to the Negro. Even before Roosevelt appointed John Collier as Indian commissioner, leaders in the Office of Indian Affairs became excited over the possibility of Indians participating in the newly formed CCC. These officials recognized that reservations badly needed forestation improvements, soil erosion control, restoration of grazing lands, and other projects envisioned for CCC, as well as employment opportunities afforded by the new program.[4]

In addition to obtaining these benefits, bureau leaders, both before and after Collier assumed office, believed firmly that the Indians should have an organization separate from the regular CCC. J. P. Kinney, director of forestry in the Indian Bureau, attended the first meetings of the CCC advisory council and pleaded for the inclusion of Indians in CCC under the control of the bureau.[5] Later Harold L. Ickes, Secretary of the Interior, took up the battle for a separate Indian program. The doughty Ickes argued in a memo to Fechner that, although reservations needed conservation work, Indians would resent the presence of white enrollees and would wish to live with their families rather than in regular CCC camps.[6]

Near the end of April 1933, President Roosevelt approved a CCC program for Indians along the lines requested by Ickes. Three days later Fechner announced that 14,400 Indians would be employed and $5,875,000 spent during the first enrollment period of six months.[7] From the first, several basic differences distinguished the Indian CCC from its parent organization. With rare exceptions, whites were not allowed to serve as enrollees. Both unmarried and married men of any

---

conditions, education, and government policy. The report revealed extreme problems on most reservations and numerous shortcomings in the federal government's conduct of Indian affairs. The commission's findings and recommendations influenced reforms made by Commissioner Charles J. Rhoads and Assistant Commissioner J. Henry Scattergood during the Hoover administration.

3 "The Social Security Act," *Indians at Work*, II (Aug. 1, 1935), 46.

4 J. P. Kinney, *Indian Forest and Range: A History of the Administration of the Redman's Heritage* (Washington, 1950), 275.

5 *Ibid.*, 275–276.

6 "Final Report of E.C.W. and C.C.C. Indian Division," 16–17, Civilian Conservation Corps-Indian Division Papers, National Archives, Record Group 75 (cited hereafter as CCC-ID, NA, RG 75).

7 *New York Times*, May 1, 1933.

age over eighteen could serve, and the general requirement for camps of 200–225 men was ignored. Camps in the Indian CCC, in fact, took any size or form that the local reservation superintendents felt suited the conditions and needs of their area. Moreover, the Office of Indian Affairs assumed the responsibility for supervision of projects, medical examinations, discipline, and camp administration.[8] Despite the free rein given to the Indian Bureau, Fechner reserved the power to disapprove expenditures of over $2,500, and to impose his own regulations if they conflicted with those of the bureau.

A more significant difference between the regular CCC and the Indian branch arose from the special role the conservation program played in achieving Collier's philosophy of handling Indian affairs. Collier's basic goals centered around Indian self-rule and called for the restoration of tribal government, a revitalization of native culture and religion, and improvement of 52,000,000 acres of Indian land so it would provide a better return. Collier's approach, especially self-rule and cultural integrity, was frequently condemned because it seemed to be at odds with the assimilation of Indians into general society. Actually, Collier hoped to revitalize and protect Indian culture for those who wished to remain on reservations, but, at the same time, he sought to equip properly those who chose to live outside.

CCC offered significant contributions to Indians regardless of which avenue they selected. For enrollees who left Indian society, work experience, new skills, and knowledge of a wage economy gained from CCC would substantially reduce the problems of adjusting to outside employment. The massive unemployment of the depression era, however, severely limited the possibility of off-reservation work, and Collier's main interest in CCC was to help the overwhelming majority of Indians who remained in their own culture. Hence, the focus of CCC in the early New Deal was to improve and conserve reservation land so more Indians would obtain at least a subsistence from farming and ranching. As a by-product of service in CCC, Collier hoped to educate Indians in improved agricultural methods and thereby increase their interest in farming and ranching. Thus, Indian CCC was tied directly to a philosophy for dealing with a minority group, while the parent organization theoretically sought only to improve the public domain without any particular reference to its present users.

While encountering delays in getting funds transferred to the In-

8 "Final Report," 7, CCC-ID, NA, RG 75.

dian Bureau, Collier created a new office in the Indian Bureau to administer the program. Jay B. Nash, a recreation expert at New York University and former associate of Collier in the American Indian Defense Association, became the initial director of the Indian CCC.[9] Both Nash and Collier sought to develop the first camps so that they mirrored local conditions and the Indians' tribal cultures. Nash spent most of the summer personally organizing camps among the Navajo and Pueblo. To handle project planning, Collier named J. P. Kinney as general production supervisor. As director of forestry in the bureau during the Hoover administration, Kinney had faced bitter criticisms from Collier and the new position was an obvious demotion. Nevertheless, Kinney remained with CCC until the program ended.

In addition to Nash's staff in Washington, Collier also established district offices to coordinate CCC projects on the reservations. These were originally located at Minneapolis, Minnesota; Muskogee, Oklahoma; Phoenix, Arizona; Spokane, Washington; Billings, Montana; and Albuquerque, New Mexico. Some of the district offices were shifted after 1933, but they still corresponded to the major geographic regions of Indian population. Each district office contained a production coordinator, foresters, engineers, camp supervisors, and draftsmen. With the exception of camp supervisors who checked on the enrollees' living conditions and off-duty activities, the district headquarters staff concerned themselves with planning and designing projects and advising field supervisors on technical problems.

Actual field work was delayed until mid-June 1933, and many reservations did not get their projects under way until July 1. By that time, fifty-six reservations had started work. The Indians' reaction to joining CCC in 1933 varied greatly from area to area. Traditional animosity for the army kept some Indians from enrolling because they understood the program would be under military control. Others refused to submit to medical examinations and vaccinations required of all new enrollees. Among the more prosperous tribes, especially the Klamaths, the Indians failed to join CCC because they retained a fairly high standard of living even in the midst of the depression. In all such cases, the bureau diverted funds to another reservation or brought in outside enrollees to work on projects. More typically, how-

---

9 John Leiper Freeman, Jr., "The New Deal for the Indians: A Study in Bureau-Committee Relations in American Government" (Ph.D. dissertation, Princeton University, 1952), 175.

ever, depression, drought, and grasshoppers broke down whatever hesitations Indians felt about CCC.[10] On some reservations they swarmed into agency headquarters to sign up. If enrollees could not be switched to another reservation, the bureau devised a system of "staggered employment" by which crews worked halftime and alternated with each other. This policy was quite widespread in 1933 as shown by a bureau estimate that 25,000 Indians worked on CCC, while the largest number hired at any one time was 13,000.[11]

Almost unbelievable confusion marked the field operations of the Indian CCC during the first work season. The already burdened superintendents assumed responsibility for recruiting, planning projects, ordering supplies, and a myriad of other tasks related to initiating field work. They frequently did not understand the purpose of CCC and selected projects unwisely. In some areas, supplies and tools were quickly exhausted from local merchants' stocks and work had to be delayed until more items arrived. Hasty planning also plagued the first year. In the Minneapolis district, for example, a forester planned all the projects for agencies of the area in less than one month.[12] Probably most jobs received no more planning than that given by an Oklahoma foreman who measured off a dam the first day and told his inexperienced crew: "Well, boys, there it is."[13]

The biggest reason for the confusion in field work in 1933 was the delay that Collier encountered in getting funds released. Most reservations started projects around July 1 and the first enrollment period was scheduled to end on September 30. Continuation of the program beyond that date depended on Roosevelt's authorization of a second enrollment period, and this seemed doubtful to officials in the Indian Bureau. Hence, Collier had to rush into haphazard arrangements to utilize funds. Even so, field work did not reach full stride until early August. At that time Collier notified the main office of the CCC that he would have $3,000,000 in unexpended funds, and he requested that the money be carried over for use in 1934.[14] Fechner relieved the

---

10 Interview with Ernest V. Downing, former agency clerk and administrator at Jicarilla, Hopi, and other agencies, Oklahoma City, March 10, 1966.

11 *Annual Report of the Secretary of the Interior, 1934* (Washington, 1934), 102–103.

12 William Heritage to District #1 Personnel, Work Plan, April 1, 1937, to June 30, 1938, CCC-ID, NA, RG 75.

13 Sylvester Tinker, "What IECW Means to the Osages," *Indians at Work*, III (Sept. 15, 1935), 18.

14 Collier to Fechner, Aug. 17, 1933, Fechner File, CCC-ID, NA, RG 75.

problem later in August when he notified Collier that the president had authorized a second enrollment period.[15]

Several important changes in the Indian CCC at the end of the first work season subsequently affected the nature of the program. Jay Nash stepped down as director and returned to New York University.[16] His replacement was Daniel Murphy, a career official in Indian Service whom Collier regarded as "one of the ablest among the old-line Bureau functionaries."[17] Collier's own role in the conservation program rapidly diminished after 1933 as he became more concerned with passing the Wheeler-Howard Act and implementing its provisions.[18] William Zimmerman, Jr., assistant commissioner, assumed more leadership as Collier became engaged elsewhere. Both Zimmerman and Murphy were careful and methodical officials who replaced the "brain trust" atmosphere of 1933 with a more deliberate administration.

A tremendous diversity characterized the project work carried out by Indian enrollees in both 1933 and later.[19] The "Final Report" of the program, in fact, lists 126 different types of projects which range from archaeological work in Arizona to the operation of a fish hatchery in Wisconsin. Nearly all production activities, however, centered around some phase of forestation, range development, or soil erosion control. Field supervisors tried to select projects on the basis of geographic conditions, the particular needs of a reservation, and the hope of providing Indians with a subsistence living. Thus the Indian CCC in the Great Lakes and Pacific Northwest regions concentrated heavily on forestation. Indian enrollees commonly built trails, cut forest lanes, and constructed lookout towers to protect the reservations' lumber resources from fires. Large tracts of timber were covered by crews who

---

15 Fechner to Collier, Aug. 22, 1933, *ibid.*

16 "Dr. Nash Completes His Task," *Indians at Work*, I (Sept. 15, 1933), 6.

17 John Collier, *From Every Zenith* (Denver, 1963), 187.

18 *U.S. Statutes at Large*, XLVII, Part I, 984–988. The Wheeler-Howard Act of 1934 was an attempt by Collier to reverse the Indian policy pursued since the Dawes Act of 1887. In the original bill, Collier sought to achieve two major ends: destruction of the allotment system, and restoration of the tribal councils as local governing units. Provisions related to dropping the allotment system and replacing it with tribal ownership of land were all defeated or weakened before the bill reached floor debate. Collier's ideas on restoring tribal government survived fairly intact. The Wheeler-Howard Act provided procedures by which tribes could establish councils. Once chartered and ratified in referendum elections, the councils served as local government units in conjunction with the Indian Service. The Wheeler-Howard Act also established revolving loan funds to finance business ventures and individuals' education.

19 The same diversity was also true of the regular CCC, although it is popularly believed that the program dwelt on forestation and tended to ignore many other important activities, such as range restoration, soil erosion control, and park development.

carried out projects to control blister rust disease and pine beetles. Equally beneficial were miles of telephone lines which the enrollees strung between lookouts and agency headquarters so fires could be detected and put out quickly.

In the northern Great Plains, the Great Basin, and the Southwest the organization concentrated on improving the Indians' grazing lands. To accomplish this, Indian enrollees eradicated rodents, threw up thousands of earth and masonry dams, drilled wells, developed springs, and reseeded range lands. One of the most helpful improvements in the Southwest was the removal of worthless and degenerate wild mustangs from the Indians' grazing lands. This project provided additional browse for sheep, goats, and cattle, but it encountered stiff resistance from many Indians who felt that the possession of horses, no matter how poor their quality, conferred prestige on their owners. Some tribes permitted the removal of the mustangs early in the New Deal, while others, most notably the Navajo and Hopi, held on to their surplus animals until the late 1930s or early 1940s.[20]

Control of soil erosion was frequently done in conjunction with range improvements. The same dams that stored water for livestock also reduced gully erosion, and a reseeded range was better able to resist the ravages of wind and drought. Soil conservation for its own sake was perhaps most prominent in Oklahoma where Indians commonly operated small farms. Enrollees of that state built check dams and terraces to stem the loss of topsoil from water runoff and set out some 200 miles of shelterbelts in western Oklahoma to prevent wind erosion.[21] The latter have now grown tall and lush and offer testimony against the mistaken idea that trees never thrive on the Great Plains.

Despite the importance of production projects, the major gains to the enrollees resulted from their life in camps. Three basic types of camps were developed in the Indian program and each reflected the needs of a particular reservation and the whims of its superintendent. The first of these, the boarding camp, came closest to resembling the installations of the regular CCC. Where work could be maintained for several years, Indian CCC officials built permanent quarters, mess halls, offices, and repair shops. The facilities at such camps were often surprisingly well equipped. Some camps possessed recreation and edu-

---

20 E. R. Fryer to Collier, April 27, 1938, CCC-ID, NA, RG 75; interview with Ernest V. Downing, March 10, 1966.

21 A. C. Monahan, "Shelterbelt Work in Kansas and Oklahoma," *Indians at Work*, V (May, 1938), 23.

cation buildings, including a gymnasium and rooms for classes in music, arithmetic, typing, and woodworking. Even less plush camps usually had a large recreation room for reading and indoor recreation. Several camps operated canteens where enrollees could buy candy, cigarettes, and sundries. Profits were used to purchase movie projectors and to rent weekly films. If work could be maintained for only a short time, boarding camps housed the enrollees in army tents with only the most rudimentary facilities. Such temporary installations were apt to be used for part of a work season and then moved to another location. The ultimate in mobility was the homemade trailer which several reservations used in making range improvements over large areas.[22]

On reservations which did not have enough unmarried enrollees, Indian CCC turned to the married camp. Such camps contained entire Indian families who lived in either tents or shacks near their work. Since the married enrollee was responsible for providing food and shelter for his entire family, he received a commutation allowance of twelve dollars per month in addition to his regular salary of thirty dollars. Such camps varied far more in quality than did the boarding installations. Some superintendents provided the Indian families with adequate housing and sanitation facilities. All too often observers reported that married camps were pestholes lacking the basic necessities for a decent life. One witness in 1936 noted that married camps in the northern Great Plains were littered with tin cans, paper, and garbage and that the Indians lacked sanitation facilities and a convenient supply of water.[23]

The third type of camp dispensed with providing housing and allowed the Indians to live at home. The enrollees met at predesignated points each morning and were picked up in CCC trucks and hauled to their projects. They received the same commutation allowance given to residents of a married camp. The arrangement had the advantage of avoiding the deplorable conditions of many boarding camps, and it allowed Indian enrollees to care for their farms on the weekends or while laid off by staggered employment. The system was most common in Oklahoma where Indians owned small farms and lived fairly close together.

---

22 "Indians in the News," *ibid.,* VI (Nov. 1938), 30; "CCC-ID on Wheels," *ibid.,* VI (Feb. 1939), 26; Klamath CCC Workers Return to Nomadic Life," *ibid.,* VIII (Oct. 1940), 33.

23 Lawrence E. Lindley, "Emergency and Relief Work," *Indian Truth,* XIII (Oct. 1936), 3.

Even more perplexing than poor camp conditions was the slowness of the Indian CCC to provide educational and rehabilitative activities for the enrollees. In part the delay may have reflected the reluctance of Fechner and the parent organization to support training programs.[24] When Fechner appeared before a House committee in 1937, he admitted that he had required only illiterates to attend education classes, and that instruction for the rest was on a voluntary basis. Fechner maintained that participants in CCC could best learn by on-the-job training rather than through formal education. The latter, he complained, was too expensive and impractical.[25] Hence, Fechner regarded CCC as primarily a work program, and he gave guarded support for education until Congress recommended ten hours of training per week in the CCC Act of 1937.[26]

In the case of the Indian CCC, stronger obstacles hampered educational activities. For some reason both local, district, and Washington leaders of the program showed greater interest in production achievements than in rehabilitation and training. Perhaps the leaders' emphasis on production stemmed from the normal bureaucratic desire to show tangible results, such as project achievements, which could be compiled in reports and tables. At any rate, most leaders of the Indian CCC claimed, like Fechner, that the program would best serve the enrollees by giving them work skills and experience. Such arguments had many merits. Most of the Indian enrollees had never held a steady job before, and working regular hours, learning how to earn and spend money, and acquiring basic skills were educational in the broadest sense. Moreover, the Indians' deplorable educational background could only have raised doubts about their ability to benefit from formal classes. Forty-eight percent of the enrollees had never attended school beyond the fourth grade, and a fairly sizeable portion were not fluent in written or spoken English.[27] The variation in types of camps, the presence of many older enrollees, and the scattered nature of project work served as additional barriers to educational activities.

The first impetus to an educational program occurred in 1934 when

---

24 An excellent summary of the education program in the CCC before 1937 is contained in John A. Salmond, *The Civilian Conservation Corps, 1933–1942* (Durham, 1967), 47–54.

25 House Committee on Labor, "Hearings on H. R. 6180, To Make Civilian Conservation Corps a Permanent Agency," 75 Cong., 1 sess. (1937), 34.

26 *U.S. Statutes at Large*, L, Part 1, 319–322.

27 "Final Report," 37, CCC-ID, NA, RG 75.

Fechner's office issued a set of safety regulations for all CCC units. These required that all production supervisors and operators of trucks and machinery be instructed in safety and first aid by men who had passed Red Cross proficiency tests. For the next two years the Indian CCC evaded full compliance with the safety and first aid program. Instruction, when given at all, was haphazardly provided by camp managers, production supervisors, and Indian Service physicians.[28]

Apparently upon pressure from Fechner's office, Daniel Murphy in late 1935 appointed Robert M. Patterson as educational director of the Indian CCC and ordered him to establish a training program for instructors of first aid and safety.[29] Before the 1936 work season, Patterson set up district training centers to which reservation superintendents sent their most outstanding and promising enrollees. Red Cross representatives instructed the classes and tested the Indian youngsters at the completion of the course.[30] The procedure for selecting enrollees in 1936 was sound, for 194 out of 211 trainees received first aid certificates and 133 out of the 194 additionally qualified as instructors.[31] The use of district training centers eventually became quite common and provided instructors in lifesaving, foremanship, fire fighting, and general safety. One unusual feature of this approach to education was that many of the enrollee instructors were required to teach in both English and their tribal tongues upon their return to home camps. Most of the instructors proved highly adept at lecturing in either of the languages.

Patterson made only minor advancements in education during the two years following the creation of the district training centers for safety and first aid. In April 1936, Assistant Commissioner William Zimmerman instructed reservation superintendents to give education a regular place in their CCC budget. Even so, training activities were to absorb only some five percent of CCC funds.[32] Patterson also seems to have drawn up preliminary plans for general training, later called the Enrollee Program, before Congress recommended ten hours of instruction for CCC in 1937. Unfortunately, he never succeeded in getting the Enrollee Program accepted in the field.

---

28 Robert M. Patterson file, Personnel Records of the Department of Interior, Federal Records Center, St. Louis, Mo.

29 Collier to all District Camp Supervisors, March 6, 1936, CCC-ID, NA, RG 75.

30 *Ibid.*

31 A. E. Demaray to Fechner, July 16, 1936, *ibid.*

32 William Zimmerman, Jr., to Superintendents and other Employees, April 6, 1936, *ibid.*

His failure again related to the strong climate of opinion among Indian CCC field leaders that the program should stress production and on-the-job training and ignore everything else. Production officials at all levels seemed to feel that formal education was a waste of time and would interfere with project work. When asked to start classes, most field leaders rationalized that education would be an excellent thing for other reservations, but their own peculiar situation unfortunately excluded any possibility for initiating a training program.

Breaking down the apathy and hostility of field leaders required the intervention of Collier. Late in 1937 or early in 1938, while visiting the Navajo reservation, Collier conferred with Claude C. Cornwall, camp supervisor of the Phoenix district office and one of the most highly respected and progressive leaders in the Indian CCC. In discussing education, Cornwall told the commissioner: "The enrollee program . . . hasn't done so well. In many places it hasn't even gotten off to a good start, and I think one of the difficulties is that some of the production staff . . . haven't given it much of a break." Cornwall went on to explain that the Indian CCC had made a commendable record in production, but it had failed miserably as an instrument of Indian rehabilitation.[33] Undoubtedly spurred by this information, Collier in late 1938 put Cornwall in charge of the Enrollee Program and transferred Patterson to the Phoenix office.[34]

After 1938, educational activities in the Indian CCC began to show surprising progress as field leaders learned that they must offer classes to the enrollees or face pressure from Washington. Cornwall's own approach to implementing the Enrollee Program followed exceedingly practical lines. He organized Enrollee Program committees on reservations and assigned them the task of planning and presenting classes to Indians in CCC. Various types of bureau employees served on the committees, including teachers, foresters, extension specialists, physicians, and CCC supervisors. Once formed, the committees selected the types of training most needed on their particular reservation, helped arrange meeting places, and frequently served as instructors. By mid-1939 Cornwall reported that fifty-nine agencies had formed Enrollee Program committees and provided an average of three hours of instruction per week for Indians on the CCC payroll.[35] Cornwall showed

33 Claude C. Cornwall to Collier, Feb. 8, 1938, *ibid.*

34 Claude C. Cornwall file, Personnel Records of the Department of Interior, Federal Records Center, St. Louis, Mo.

35 D. E. Murphy to Superintendents, Oct. 25, 1939, CCC-ID, NA, RG 75.

a year later that Indian enrollees had received nearly four hours of instruction per week during the previous twelve months.[36]

The types of subject matter provided under the Enrollee Program can only be outlined, but most of the classes were extremely practical and were closely related to project work. Thus, enrollees commonly learned the operation and maintenance of trucks and heavy machinery, methods of fighting forest fires, surveying land, various aspects of soil conservation, and improved farming and ranching techniques. Cornwall encouraged supervisors to take time off from work and provide instruction at the project sites. In building a masonry dam, for example, the foreman in charge was to explain why the project was needed, and how to mix mortar and use the tools properly. Cornwall even provided a four-step plan of instruction for on-the-job training which included telling enrollees what to do, demonstrating how to do it, letting the Indians do the work themselves, and criticizing their performance. When handled by an astute and willing foreman, on-the-job training provided definite benefits to the enrollees, even on the remote and isolated reservations of the Southwest and the Great Basin.

Undoubtedly the most ingenious feature of the Enrollee Program in the two regions was a mobile "classroom" which the Phoenix office set up in 1939. The classroom in reality was a panel truck equipped with a movie projector, films, portable generator, books, and audiovisual materials. A teacher in charge traveled from one CCC camp to another and taught classes on conservation.[37] At night he showed films to the enrollees and to curious interlopers who sometimes traveled for miles on foot, horseback, or in ancient jalopies to a free movie. The Navajo, in particular, seemed completely obsessed by the movies. Their interest in the films remained undampened even when shown long conservation movies depicting blowing sand and dust storms that all had experienced firsthand. In a similar vein, even though most of the audience knew only a smattering of English, the Navajo were completely fascinated by Hollywood productions with involved and complex plots. Of the numerous stories about the Navajos' reactions to movies, perhaps the most humorous concerned one group who emptied a hogan in record time when a projector suddenly flashed a close-up of a locomotive roaring under a full head of steam.[38]

---

36 D. E. Murphy to all Superintendents, Sept. 1, 1940, *ibid.*
37 Claude C. Cornwall to Collier, May 18, 1939, *ibid.*
38 "Indians in the News," *Indians at Work*, IX (Dec. 1941), 18.

Other districts developed their own approaches and methods in the Enrollee Program. The reservations in the Minneapolis district emphasized the three R's during the winter months so the enrollees could master enough subject matter to pass state tests certifying them as eighth-grade graduates. Such classes were taught by Works Progress Administration instructors. After failing miserably to interest enrollees in off-duty activities, Oklahoma finally stumbled onto a "voluntary overtime procedure" in creating an educational program. Under this plan the Indians worked one hour overtime Monday through Thursday and, in return, they received Friday afternoons off for classes on various subjects. The popularity and flexibility of the "voluntary overtime procedure" soon led to its adoption in many other regions where the enrollees lived at home or in married camps. In Washington and Idaho the district camp manager made arrangements with the state departments of education and WPA for enrollees to take correspondence courses which could be used for high school or college credit. The enrollees showed considerable initial interest in the courses, but after their enthusiasm waned, the camp manager organized classes in mechanics at Indian CCC shops.

After an agonizingly slow start, education in the Indian CCC had by 1940 gained a prominent place in the organization. No longer could the Indian CCC be characterized as strictly a production program. Once in operation, the Enrollee Program struck a compromise by providing some classes which were closely related to project work and other instruction which was aimed at rehabilitation.

While education was gaining more attention, production activities of the Indian CCC faced serious difficulties from fund cuts as World War II approached. An indication of retrenchment occurred in late 1937 when President Roosevelt and Fechner reviewed the budget for the coming year. The President asked that Fechner freeze the number of salaried personnel in CCC as a first step in a retrenchment of the program.[39] A month later, Fechner established a ratio policy on funds for all units of CCC. The order stated that supervisors must employ one enrollee for each $930 received in CCC funds, and the ratio was made retroactive to the start of fiscal 1938 even though half the year had passed.[40]

The new fiscal ruling struck particularly hard at the Indian CCC

39 Conrad L. Wirth to Burlew, Nov. 9, 1937, CCC-ID, NA, RG 75.
40 D. E. Murphy to Superintendents and Field Men, Dec. 15, 1937, *ibid.*

because the organization had normally hired more supervisors and employed more machinery on projects than other units of the parent organization. It was quickly apparent that in the future the costs of enrollee wages, room, and board would absorb roughly 60 percent of CCC funds. The remaining 40 percent had to bear the expense of supervision, production materials, transportation, machinery, and all other items. Projects which used machinery clearly had to be cut back, and this often meant stopping the most essential work. The Navajo reservation, for example, was in the midst of an extensive program of drilling deep wells and erecting huge water storage tanks when Fechner imposed the $930 limitation. Both wells and tanks were vital to the tribe's livestock industry, but they conflicted with the new ruling since nearly all the CCC money was spent on machinery and materials and very little went to enrollees. The same was true of many other projects, especially the construction of large dams for irrigation.

The nature of project work changed considerably after Fechner ordered the $930 limitation. Field supervisors designed more projects which used hand work and ignored those which demanded machinery. In other instances, the Indian CCC evaded the ratio ruling by entering into cooperative agreements with another relief agency or division of the Indian Bureau to complete projects jointly. It became commonplace on reservations for CCC to provide labor and supervision while another agency assumed the expense of machinery, materials, and gasoline. Badly affected by the ratio were agencies with worn-out machinery, but even worse off were small reservations in the Southwest. The latter always faced a high overhead in supervisory and technical personnel and could not employ hand labor for their most productive work—digging wells, building dams, and bulldozing trails. Regardless of the field workers' hardships and complaints, the ratio system of allotting funds remained in force until the CCC went out of existence.

Coupled with Fechner's limitations on spending were serious reductions in funds for operating the Indian CCC during its last years. The first reduction came in fiscal 1939 when Fechner slashed the budget by slightly over $1 million. In fiscal 1940, the Indian CCC received about the same amount, but the next year suffered another $1 million reduction.[41] The first cut seemingly did not harm the program except to pare away nonessential spending. The second reduction, however, was coupled with a new ratio limitation of $830 and imposed

---

41 "Civilian Conservation Corps Program of the United States Department of the Interior," Jan. 1944, *ibid.* (summary report).

genuine hardships on the Indian CCC. No doubt rising prices added to the problem. Some field leaders reported in 1941 and 1942 that they could not feed the enrollees properly with their current funds, while others complained that the $930 limitation did not permit worth-while projects to be undertaken. Moreover, the draft and activation of reserve officers removed several key supervisors and further endan-gered the program. At best, the Indian CCC struggled to survive dur-ing its last two years.

Fortunately, the opportunities for Indian enrollees brightened enormously while the conservation program encountered its most serious problems. The Enrollee Program received a significant boost from the National Defense Vocational Training Act when Indians were ruled eligible for its benefits early in 1941.[42] Collier immediately decided that CCC enrollees would receive most of the training under the new program. Thanks to the Enrollee Program, camp supervisors required little time to launch national defense classes in radio opera-tion and repair, carpentry, welding, sheet metal work, auto mechanics, and similar subjects. The classes were paid for by the national govern-ment and offered in cooperation with state departments of education. Indian enrollees attended the courses for three hours a day and most instruction lasted six to eight weeks. After completing the course, all participants took proficiency tests which, if passed, almost automat-ically guaranteed employment in defense work. The Indian CCC sponsored forty-three classes for 932 enrollees with national defense funds.[43]

The national defense classes and experience in the Indian CCC al-lowed hundreds of former enrollees to find off-reservation jobs during 1941 and 1942. Incomplete studies of job placement for enrollees dur-ing the late 1930s indicate that few were able to find private employ-ment. It was fairly common for enrollees to advance to supervisory jobs in the CCC and other relief agencies or to permanent positions in the Indian Service, but few entered private employment. A systematic study of job placement in mid-1940 revealed the start of a new trend. The study showed that some 2,000 enrollees out of 7,300 had left the program during the previous year. Approximately 600 had found private jobs, 1,000 had returned to self-employment, and the re-mainder had entered the Indian Service.[44]

42 J. W. Studebaker to Executive Officers, Jan. 28, 1941, *ibid.*
43 "Final Report," 35, *ibid.*
44 D. E. Murphy to Collier, Aug. 13, 1940, *ibid.*

The trend for enrollees to enter private employment in 1940 grew rapidly during the next two years. Records of the period repeatedly show Indians leaving reservations and moving to urban centers where they earned ten dollars per day or higher in defense work. The former enrollees commonly served as welders, sheet metal workers, mechanics, machinists, or in semiskilled tasks such as truck driving. Most had learned their trade in the Indian CCC and other relief work.

The hiring of Navajos in 1941 to build a new ordnance depot at Fort Wingate, New Mexico, provides an interesting example of Indians using their new employment opportunities. The colorful Navajo, many of whom were strong "blanket" types, quickly demonstrated that they could handle construction work. "Army officers and contractors at the project," wrote a local reporter, "wondered where so many of the Navajo workmen learned to operate tractors, trucks, and perform so well as skilled carpenters and stone masons. The answer," the reporter continued, "is that the Civilian Conservation Corps program on the Reservation for the past eight years has enabled many Navajo so inclined to learn those occupations."[45] The Navajos' cultural trait of changing their names frequently threw the payroll at Fort Wingate into chaos. They also learned how to cope with abusive white bosses. Each foreman started with an equal-sized gang of Indians each morning, but the Navajo slipped quietly away from disliked bosses at every opportunity. At the end of the day, some gangs had doubled or tripled in size, while only a handful of Indians remained in others. Despite their quirks, the Navajo proved adaptive and willing workers.

The period between American entry into World War II and the termination of CCC brought a brief but drastic change in the nature of projects carried on by enrollees who remained in the Indian CCC. The enrollees sometimes helped in establishing military camps in early 1942, and all boarding installations planted victory gardens and participated in campaigns to buy war bonds and stamps. The stream of Indians leaving reservations to enter war industry was joined by hundreds of others who left for the armed services. An estimated 11,000 Indians were in the military by the end of 1942, and approximately 6,400 of these were former enrollees. Another 8,000 Indians were working in war industry at the same time.[46]

---

45 *Gallup Independent,* June 18, 1941.
46 *New York Times,* Dec. 22, 1942; "Final Report," 25, CCC-ID, NA, RG 75.

Even though the CCC offered new opportunities to Indians during its last two years, Congress abruptly terminated the entire program on July 2, 1942.[47] Precise details on the disbanding of the Indian CCC are lacking because the federal government transferred the Office of Indian Affairs to Chicago in the same period and few records were kept during the final months. On July 10, Daniel Murphy directed field supervisors to halt the project work so that CCC property could be transferred to other government agencies.

The Murphy order ended a program which deeply affected Indians for over nine years. More than 85,000 had served in the CCC and over seventy reservations had received $72,000,000 in conservation funds. In terms of physical improvements, the program had produced sizeable results. To cite a few achievements, Indian forests had benefited from 9,739 miles of truck trails, 1,315,870 acres of pest control, and 91 lookout towers. Indian grazing and farm lands had also been aided by such projects as 263,129 acres of poisonous weed eradication, 12,230 miles of fencing, and 1,742 large dams and reservoirs.[48] Probably at no time before or since have Indian forests and lands been in better condition than in 1942.

The results of such physical achievements, however, did not bring uniform economic improvements to all reservations. Undoubtedly, reservations with low population levels and large tracts of good grazing land benefited most of all. Fencing out white ranchers' strays, water development, and reseeding helped to raise sales of Indian cattle from $263,095 in 1933 to $3,126,326 by 1939.[49] Other policies and programs of the Collier administration unrelated to the CCC also contributed to the increase: acquisition of cattle, discouragement of leasing to white ranchers, introduction of registered bulls, loans for foundation stock, and organization of Indian cattlemen's associations.

Increased revenues from forests were slower and less easily achieved than those from range improvement projects. This was not due to a lack of attention to forestation, but because most Indian lumber resources were too remote to be cut profitably unless prices were high. The various improvements and protection from fire began to produce benefits only after the economy revived and wartime demands raised

---

47 *U.S. Statutes at Large*, LVI, Part 1, 569.
48 "Final Report," 71–74, CCC-ID, NA, RG 75.
49 "Hard Riding Cowboys Combine Old Skills with Modern Methods to Make Cattle Business Pay," *Indians at Work*, VIII (Dec. 1940), 7–10.

lumber prices. In fiscal 1941 Indians received $1,835,000 from lumber sales and similar figures were recorded during war years.[50]

The Indian CCC had a limited economic impact on reservations which were suitable only for grazing and which had been unwisely allotted by the Dawes Commission. An intensive study of the Lower Brule (South Dakota) in 1937 offers a depressing example of the ineffectiveness of land improvement on this type of reservation. The study group found that the residents derived only 18 percent of their income from agriculture as compared to 50 percent from the CCC and other relief agencies. Even more striking was the fact that relief programs operated at odds with Collier's goal of interesting Indians in subsistence farming and ranching. Relief work had attracted fifty-five of ninety-six Indian families away from their land. Just as the distribution of rations had drawn Indians together in the nineteenth century, the offering of relief jobs caused residents at Lower Brule to cluster near the agency headquarters. The shacks and tents used for summer residence became permanent homes despite the terrible winters in the area.[51] The obvious conclusion to be drawn from the Lower Brule and similar reservations is that the CCC could not really be effective, except as a dole, until the allotment system was destroyed and adequate land resources were given to Indians.

Even though the public has always accepted CCC publicity which stressed the program's wholesome effects on enrollees, we have no conclusive evidence that these assertions are true on a long-range basis. We badly need careful follow-up studies of former enrollees' careers before any accurate assessment can be made about the social effects of the CCC. Such studies might well reveal that the program had much less rehabilitative effect than is commonly believed. In the case of the Indian enrollees, the impact of the CCC is complicated by their minority status in American society. The obstacles faced by Indians made the benefits of the CCC—improved morale, better adjustment to changing conditions, and acquisition of work skills—much more important for Indians than for whites. Unfortunately, we do not have sufficient data on the subsequent careers of former Indian enrollees to be able to determine whether service in the CCC greatly benefited them.

Available evidence indicates that the Indian CCC had its greatest

---

50 *Annual Report of the Secretary of the Interior, 1941* (Washington, 1941), 428.

51 Allen G. Harper, "Salvaging the Wreckage of Indian Allotments," in Oliver La-Farge, ed., *The Changing Indian* (Norman, 1942), 89–95.

impact on younger and better-educated enrollees. White supervisors understandably gave such youngsters more attention, promoted them to higher jobs, and sent them to district instructor schools. Far more than older participants, the younger Indians were adaptable and willing to seize their opportunities and apply them to off-reservation employment. Moreover, most young Indian enrollees, even more than whites of the same age, were at a crossroads during the 1930s. Service in the CCC gave Indian youngsters a chance to find themselves, to mature, and to learn a trade rather than submit to apathy and despair.

It seems most doubtful that many young Indian enrollees stayed on the land as farmers and ranchers, as Collier had hoped, because many reservations, like the Lower Brule, simply did not have the resources to provide even a subsistence living. Moreover, such factors as lack of capital, the allotment system of land tenure, white prejudice, alcoholism, poor health, and other problems have plagued Indians since 1942 little less than in earlier periods. Like all people, Indians find the road to success hard to travel when no road exists. The absence of local opportunities prompted the exodus from the poorer reservations, and there is evidence that those who left have never returned unless forced by serious circumstances. Ironically, a conservation program designed to improve Indian land probably had its greatest impact in permitting former enrollees to take up careers in industrial centers.

Index

Aboriginal peoples
  Australia, 27 passim, 29n
  Conference of, *F*
  Fourth World movement, *F*
  New Guinea, 27–53
Acculturation, 36–37, 56, 63–76, 103–126,
  129, 141, 144. *See also* Wilbur R.
  Jacobs, "The Fatal Confrontation,"
  27–53
  Stages of, 17–18
Adams, C. E., 89–90
Adams, Hank, *F*
Adams, John, 42
Addington, J. P., 91
Agriculture. *See* Farming
Akwesasne Notes, 76
Alaska, 11–12, 53
Alcoholism, *F*, 37, 45, 144. *See also* Nancy
  O. Lurie, "The World's Oldest On-
  Going Protest Demonstration," 55–76
  Alternatives to, 70–76
  As form of protest, 55 passim, 64, 75
  Indian legislation against, 61
Algonquin, 28n
Almquist, Alan J., 16
American Indian Defense Association, 130
American Indian Historical Society, 22
American Society for Ethnohistory, 16
Anthropological studies, 12–18, 102–103.
  See also Ethnohistory
Apache, 39, 78 passim
Appalachia, 43n
Arapaho, 78, 83, 99n
Archaeology and the CCC, 132
Arizona, 15, 130, 132, 137
Arthur, George (Lt. Governor, Australia),
  43
Assimilation, 10, 36–39, 46, 49, 53, 101–
  103, 105, 129,141, 144
Australia. *See* Wilbur R. Jacobs, "The
  Fatal Confrontation," 27–53;
  Aboriginal peoples

Bailey, Joseph, 97–98
Bands, 114. *See also* Social structure

Banyaca, Thomas, *F*
Basques, *F*
Benton, Thomas Hart, 42
Berkhofer, Robert F., Jr., *F*, 18, 101–126
  ("The Political Context of a New
  Indian History")
Black civil rights movement, 58
Blacks, 58, 127. *See also* Aboriginal
  peoples
  Australian, 44–45
Black River Falls Banner-Journal, 72
Blackfeet, 15, 105n
Brandon, William, 4, 46
Bretons, *F*
Brown, Dee, *F*
Buffalo, 81–82. *See also* Hunting
Burnett, Samuel Bark, 78–80, 83, 85n, 91,
  93–94, 96–99

Calhoun, John C., 42, 46
California Indians, 16, 30n–31n, 37n,
  40–41, 114
Canada, *F*, 30n, 50, 69, 74
Cash, Joseph H., 25
Cass, Lewis, 43
Catawba, 105n
Cattlemen, *F*, 77 passim
Cattle industry. *See* Grazing range;
  Ranching
Cherokee, 18, 19n, 49n, 50, 105n, 108–112,
  115, 116n, 118–19, 118n, 122
Cherokee Commission, 92
Cherokee Strip, 89
Cheyenne, 19, 78, 83, 99
Chickasaw, 24, 79, 81, 83
Chiefs. *See* Leadership
Chippewa, 66n. *See also* Ojibwa
Choctaw, 122
Civilian Conservation Corps (CCC), *F*,
  127 passim
Clayton, Reverend John, 47
Climate. *See* Ecological adaptation
Clinard, Marshall, 57
Cloud, Charles R. (Charley) Lowe, 72
Cobb, Colonel J. D., 93

Collier, John, 128–32, 136–37, 140, 142
Comanche, 77 passim
Comanche Jack (Permansu), 85–86
Conservation, 27–28, 28n
    CCC, 127 passim
Constitution of the Five Nations, 38
Contra-acculturation, 37. *See also*
    Acculturation
Cook, Captain James, 30–31, 30n
Cook, Warren L., 24
Cooper, John N., 28n
Corkran, David H., 109–112
Cornwall, Claude C., 137–38
Costo, Rupert, 22
Creek, 112n
Criminality, 62, 62n
Crow, 78
Curtis, Charles, 97
Custer, General George, 20

Dampier, William, 44
Dams, 131, 133, 137, 140, 142
Dawes Commission, 143
Dawes Severalty Act (1887), 92
Day, George D., 90, 92
Debo, Angie, 4
Degérando, Joseph-Marie, 16–17
Delaware, 14, 38, 116, 116n, 124n
Delaware Prophet, 38n
Deloria, Vine, Jr., *F*, 20–21, 25, 59n, 75,
    106n
Disease, 28, 32–33, 33n, 37, 45, 65n, 144
Dispossession, *F*, 33–34, 38, 47, 50–51, 50n
    Justifications for, 42–43
Dogrib, 69, 70–72, 74
Downing, Ernest V., 131n
Dozier, Edward P., 15, 18, 61
Driver, Harold E., 12–13
Drunkenness. *See* Alcoholism
Dutch (New Guinea), 35

Ecological adaptation, 27–29, 31–32, 51
Edgerton, Robert, 55–56, 65, 67
Education, 135, 139, 141. *See also*
    Training and Rehabilitation
Elites, 122
Elkin, A. P., 29n, 37, 47
Employment, 129, 141–42
Enrollee Program (CCC), 136–40
Eskimo, 4, 11, 53
Ethnohistory, 10–18, 24, 104, 106, 125n
Expansion, white, 28, 36, 39, 43n, 46, 51
Expertise, 71–73
Exploitation, 35, 41, 78, 80–99
Express (Chickasha), 93
Extermination, *F*, 9, 101–102

Tasmania, 43–45
Ewers, John C., 15, 19

Factionalism, tribal, 85–92, 99, 109–110,
    117–24. *See also* Intertribal relations
Farb, Peter, 4, 116
Farming, 28n, 50, 92, 129, 133–34, 137,
    142–44
Fechner, Robert, 127–29, 131, 134, 139–40
Fenton, William N., 3, 15, 28n, 119
Fey, Harold E., 5
Fiedler, Leslie A., 9
Firefighting, 132, 136–37
Fisheries, 132
Flemish, *F*
Flood, W. W., 90
Flynn, Dennis, 93
Folsom, Paris H., 86
Forestry, 128, 132, 137, 142
Fort Sill, Oklahoma, 78–99
Fort Wingate, New Mexico, 141–42
Fourth World, *F*, 54
Fox, Chief Red, *F*
Fox, George W., 86
Franklin, Benjamin, 32n
Frederick, Jack, 18
Frontier, 7–8, 10, 24, 27 passim, 35–36, 46,
    77, 112n
    Theory (Turner thesis), 51–52
Fur trading, 28n, 50

Gearing, Frederick O., 109–112, 115
Germans (New Guinea), 34–35
Gipps, Sir George (Governor, Australia),
    45
Georgia, 50
Ghost Dance, 19
Gibson, Arrell M., 5, 24
Gibson, Charles, 17
Grass money, 87–92, 99
Grazing range, 80 passim, 128, 132–33,
    142–43. *See also* Cattlemen; Ranching
Great Binding Law, 38
Great Lakes Indians, 65n
Greek Orthodox Church, 12
Greer County, 79, 82

Hagan, William T., *F*, 5–6
Hall, J. Lee, 87–88
Hallowell, Alfred Irving, 10
Handsome Lake, 14–15, 37–38, 62, 62n,
    126. *See also* Religious movements
Hano, 15
Haryana, 117n
Hawaiians, 66–67. *See also* Pacific
    islanders

Heidenreich, Conrad E., 28n
Heizer, Robert F., 16
Henry, Jeannette, 22
Henry, Major Guy V., 82–83
Herring, C. T., 91
Hill, James J., *F*
Hinton, Thomas B., 16–17
Historiography. *See* Wilcomb Washburn,
  "The Writing of American Indian
  History," 3–25; Robert F. Berkhofer,
  "The Political Context of a New
  Indian History," 101–126
Ho-Dé-No-Sau-Nee, 119n
Hogbin, Ian, 11
Homesteaders, 93, 95–98
Hoover, Herbert T., 25
Hopi, *F*, 131n, 133
Hordes, 41. *See also* Social structure
Horticulturalists, 33
Howling Wolf, 19
Hubbard, William, 7, 7n
Hudson's Bay Company, 50, 50n
Hunt, P. B., 81–87
Hunting, 28, 28n, 81–82
Huron Indians, 28n, 105n, 123n

Ickes, Harold L., 128
Idaho, 139
Indian identity, 56, 64, 69–70, 102,
  106–107, 116
Indian literature, 21
Indian policy
  British, 46, 112n, 123
  Canadian, 50
  Colonial powers, 17, 24
  Early American, 6–7, 24
  Jacksonian, 6
  Jeffersonian, 24
  Puritan, 7
  U.S. reservation policy, 77–99
Indian publications, 76–93
Indian Reorganization Act, 116
Indian scholars, *F*, 15, 20–22, 25
Indian wars, *F*, 7–8, 45n, 46, 49, 78. *See
  also* King Philip's War; Pequot War;
  Pontiac's uprising
Indian-white relations, *F*, 18, 101–102,
  110
  Discrimination, 16, 76, 127
  Federal government's role (reserva-
    tion policy), 6, 53, 76n, 77 passim
  Historiography, 3, 5–6, 14
  Impact of Indians on whites, 8–10,
    54n
  Impact of whites on Indians, 9, 13,
    36–37, 39, 77, 115–16, 123

Influence of law, 22, 94
  Perpetuation of distinction, 64. *See
    also* Racism; Segregation
  Trade, 6, 68–69
  Treaties and Agreements: (1868), *F*;
    Canada, 6, 25, 74; (1970), 76n;
    (1867), 77–78, 77n; (1838), 119
Intertribal relations, 31–32, 85, 124–25.
  See also Factionalism
Irish, *F*
Iroquois, 4, 14–15, 32n, 38, 68n, 105n, 114,
  115n–116n, 118–19, 118n
Isatai, 85–86
Isleta Pueblo, 118n

Jackson, Andrew. *See* Indian policy
Jacobs, Wilbur R., *F*, 6, 27–53 ("The
  Fatal Confrontation: Early Native-
  White Relations on the Frontiers of
  Australia, New Guinea, and America—
  A Comparative Study")
Jefferson, Thomas. *See* Indian policy;
  Indian-white relations
Jennings, Jesse D., 13
Jerome Agreement, 92–94, 99
Jerome, David, 92
Jicarilla, 131n
Johnson, Sir William, 48
Jones, Henry Mumford, 9
Jorgensen, Joseph G., 24
Joseph, Chief, *F*
Josephy, Alvin M., Jr., *F*, 4–5, 126, 126n

Kansa, 24
Kansas, 80–81, 133n
Kaw, 89
Kickapoo, 5
Kilpatrick, Anna Gritts, 18
King Philip's War (1676), 7–8, 7n
Kinney, J. P., 128, 128n, 130
Kiowa, 21, 77 passim
Kiowa-Apaches, 78, 96
Klamath, 105, 130, 134n
Knight, Rolf, 28n
Kroeber, Alfred L., 28n, 29, 31n, 39, 41
Kroeber, Clifton B., 10

Lafitau, Joseph-Francois, 15
Lamar, Lucius Q., 86–87
Land. *See also* Dispossession
  Allotments, 92, 95–96, 99n, 143n, 144
  Ethic, 31, 51
  Expansion, white, *F*, 28, 30, 34, 36,
    51. *See also* Expansion, white
  Importance to Indians, 29, 143
  Improvement, 128–29, 132–33, 137,

142–43. *See also* Civilian Conservation Corps
  Leasing, *F*, 82–99
  Tenure, 28n, 31n, 34, 36, 42, 115n
Language, 33, 70–71, 136, 138
Leach, Douglas, 6–8
Leacock, Eleanor, 14, 28n
Leadership, Indian, 37, 68, 73, 99, 109, 115, 122
  Corruption of, 85, 90, 92–94, 99, 110
Leopold, Aldo, 31
Liberty, Margot, 19
Linton, Ralph, 59, 117
Liquor. *See* Alcoholism
Locke, John, 44
Lone Wolf, 89n, 90, 92
Longhouse (Handsome Lake Church), 38
Lurie, Nancy Oestreich, *F*, 14, 47, 55–76, 101n, ("The World's Oldest On-Going Protest Demonstration: North American Indian Drinking Patterns")

MacAndrew, Craig, 55–56, 65, 67
Mackenzie, General Ranald, 80
Macleod, William Christy, 46
Magnet (Marlow), 93
Malinowski, Bronislaw, 11
Malone, Henry, 109–112
Manuel, Chief George, *F*
Maoris, 37, 44
Marsden, Reverend Samuel, 44
Martin, Calvin, 54n
Marx, Leo, 8
Massacres, 8, 35, 45n
Mather, Increase, 7, 7n
McGuire, Bird S., 98
McNickle, D'Arcy, 5
Menominees, *F*
Menomini, 37n, 105n
Meriam Commission, 127, 127n
Midiwin, 105n
Militancy, *F*, 20, 58, 76
Mining, 28, 39, 47
Minnesota, 130–31, 138
Minorities Rights Group, 54n
Minstrel (Minco), 93
Missions and Missionaries, 12, 37n, 45, 63, 120n, 122n. *See also* Protestants; Religion
Missouri, 83–84
Momaday, Scott, *F*, 21
Montana, 130
Morality, 21
Moravian Church, 12
Morgan, Lewis Henry, 119

Mountain Wolf Woman, 70
Movies and films, 138
Murphy, Daniel, 132, 136, 139n, 141n, 142
Mustangs, 133
Myers, William D., 88
Myth, 8–9, 23, 25, 32

Napaskiak, 11
Nash, Jay B., 130, 132
National Congress of American Indians, 21, 76, 124
National Defense Vocational Training Act (1941), 140
National Indian Youth Council, 124
Nationalism, 105, 109
  Pseudo-nationalism, 110
Native American Church, 62, 62n. *See also* Peyote religion
Nativist movements, 53
Navajo, 38–39. 65n, 66n, 115–16, 116n, 130, 133, 137–39, 141
Navajo Community College, 22
Negroes. *See* Blacks
New Deal, CCC and WPA, 127 passim
New England, 7
New Guinea, 27 passim. *See also* 27n–53n for bibliography
New Mexico, 130, 141
New York, 14–15
Nez Perce, 5, 105n, 118, 118n, 120n, 121n
Nomads, 33, 41–42, 44, 48, 78
North Carolina, 19n, 116n
Northeastern Indians, 28n, 38, 54n, 115n

Oglala, *F*. *See also* Sioux
Ohio, 103n
Ojibwa, 57, 57n, 63, 68–69, 69n. *See also* Chippewa
Oklahoma, 4, 77 passim, 92–93, 98, 130–31, 133–34
Oliver, Douglas L., 28n, 29n
Olson, James C., 5
Oneida (Iroquois), 118n
Oral history, 18–23, 25, 119, 120n
Ortiz, Alfonso, 15
Osage, 78, 131n
Oswalt, Wendell H., 11–12
Otoe, 89
Ottawa, 38

Pacific islanders, 27 passim, 29n, 53n, 66–67, 67n
Pacific Northwest, *F*, 5, 24, 69, 112
Paleo Indians, 28n
Pan-Indianism, 101, 105

Papago, 64n
Papua-New Guinea. *See* New Guinea
Parker, Arthur C., 15, 119n
Parker, Cynthia, 85
Parman, Donald L., *F*, 127–44 ("The
 Indian and the Civilian Conservation
 Corps")
Patterson, Robert M., 136–37
Pawnee, 78
Pearce, Roy Harvey, 8
Peckham, Howard, 17
Pennsylvania, 14
Penobscot, 28n
Pequot War (1637), 7
Permansu. *See* Comanche Jack
Petersen, Karen Daniels, 19
Peyote religion, 62, 62n, 70, 124, 124n
Philip, King, 8. *See also* King Philip's
 War
Place-names, 31n
Plains Indians, *F*, 15, 19, 38, 69, 77
 passim, 115, 133
Pocahontas, 9
Political behavior, 101 passim
Political process, 108–126
Political structure, 113–15, 117–26
Pontiac's uprising (1763), 38, 38n, 46, 49
Pope, Major General John, 84
Population, 32–33, 39–40, 40n, 54n
Potawatomi, 56n, 63n, 118n
Poverty, 45, 65n, 127, 144
Prejudices. *See also* Racism
 Influence on Indian history and
  historiography, 11, 22–23, 46–49,
  75, 108, 111, 116–17, 127, 144
Prophet Dance, 105n
Protest, 101
 Alcoholism, 55 passim
 Red Power movement, 20, 101
Protestants, 18, 120n. *See also* Missions
 and Missionaries
Prucha, Francis Paul, 6–7
Pueblo Indians, 15, 18, 39, 118, 118n, 130

Quam, Alvina, 25
Quanah, 85–86, 88, 90, 92, 94, 99

Racism, 46–47, 50, 127. *See also* Prejudices
Railroads, *F*, 47
Ranching, 129, 137, 139, 142–44. *See also*
 Grazing range
Randlett, James D., 96
Rations, 78, 80–81, 83–84, 94
Rave, John, 62n
Red Cloud, 5

Red Cross, 135–36
Red Power movement, 20, 101
Redfield, Robert, 122
Rehabilitation. *See* Education; Training
 and Rehabilitation
Religion, 24, 105n, 125n. *See also*
 Missions and Missionaries; Peyote
 religion
Religious movements, 24, 38, 62, 62n, 70,
 124. *See also* Handsome Lake
Reservations, 24, 45, 47, 50n
 Cattlemen and government policy,
  77 passim
 CCC, 128 passim
Rhoads, Charles J., 128n
Rogers, Robert, 48
Roosevelt, Franklin Delano, 131, 139
Roosevelt, Theodore, 43
Russian traders, 12

Sac and Fox Indians, 5
Sand Creek, *F*
Santa Clara Pueblo, 105n
Savages, 8–9, 16–17, 44n
Scattergood, J. Henry, 128
Segregation. *See also* Reservations
 CCC, 77–78, 98–99, 127–28
Self-determination, 49, 129
Seneca, 14–15, 37–39, 68n, 118n, 119
Service, Elman R., 4
Settlers. *See* Homesteaders
Shamans, 18
Sheehan, Bernard W., 9, 25
Shelley, W. C., 94
Sheridan, General Philip, 83
Shoshone, 27, 78
Silberstein, Asher, 96
Sioux, 5, 19, 60n, 61–62, 61n–62n
Sitting Bull, 19
Slotkin, Richard, 25
Smith, Henry Nash, 8–9
Smith, Hoke, 93
Social structure, 13, 29, 41, 68, 107–110,
 113–15, 122
 Examples, 70–76
Sorcery, 32, 35, 65n
South America, *F*
South Carolina, 49n
South Dakota, *F*, 25, 143
Southwest Indians, 13, 29n
Speck, Frank G., 28n
Spencer, Robert F., 13
Spicer, Edward H., 13, 17, 29n, 123
Squaw men, 81, 81n, 94–95, 94n, 99
Stands in Timber, John, 19

Steen, Sheila C., 15
Steiner, Stanley, 20, 101n
Stephens, James J., 98
Stereotypes, Indian, 46–49, 57–58, 65n, 76,
    112
    Tribal, 124
    White, 62
Stocking, George, Jr., 17
Students, Indian, 64
Sugg, E. C., 83, 86, 91, 94, 96–99
Sun Dance, 24
Sweden, *F*

Tabananaka, 85, 87–88
Tasmania, 40, 42–44, 45
Teedyuscung, 14
Teller, Henry M., 84–85
Ten Bears, 85
Tewa, 15
Texas, 77 passim
Timber barons, *F*
Tobacco, 67
Tonawanda, 119n
Totemism, 31–32
Training and Rehabilitation, 127, 129,
    134–39, 140–44. *See also* Education
Treaties. *See* Indian-white relations
Tribal identity, *F*, 63, 107. *See also* Indian
    identity
Trobrianders, 11
Trollope, Anthony, 44
Tsembaga, 30n
Turner, Frederick Jackson, 51

Unrau, William E., 24
Utes, 45n
Utley, Robert M., 19

Values, Indian, 66–76
Vaughan, Alden, 6–7
Vestal, Stanley, 19
Violence, 24, 62–63

Virginia, 47

Waggoner, Daniel, 78–80, 83, 85n, 90–91,
    93
Waggoner, William T., 94, 96–99
Walapai, 115n
Wallace, Anthony F. C., 14–15, 126
Wampanoag, 8
Warfare, 78
War on Poverty, *F*
Washburn, Wilcomb, *F*, 3–25 ("The
    Writing of American Indian History:
    A Status Report")
Washington, 130, 138
Wells, 133, 139–40
Welsh, *F*
Wheeler-Howard Act (1934), 132, 132n
White, E. E., 88
White, Leslie A., 4
White Man, 90
White Wolf, 85, 92
Whites, *See* Expansion, white; Exploita-
    tion; Extermination; Indian-white
    relations
Whittaker, J. O., 61
Wichita, 89
Williams, Roger, 48
Winnebago, 69, 72–73
Winthrop, John, 43
Wirt, William, 50
Wisconsin, 37n, 69, 105, 132
Wissler, Clark, 12
Witchcraft, 32, 35, 65n
Wolftown, 18, 19n, 116n
Works Progress Administration, 138–39
World War II, 139, 141–42
Wounded Knee, *F*
Wyman, Walker D., 10

Zimmerman, William, Jr., 132, 136
Zuni, 25